WHEN I WALK THROUGH

me. I wonder what motivated the author when they were creating their cover. What message did they want to convey?

As I was writing "Through the Eyes of Guilt", the idea for the cover seemed to unfold and formulate in my mind over a few months. My first brush was drawn towards what our eyes convey about life - how we see and experience life, and the reactions and responses we embrace. But there needed to be more to the image than just "eyes".

In my mind, the cover would encompassed what we experience during our life, how our lives could offer us much more than we could ever imagine, how to experience life to its fullest and how everything that comes our way leaves its mark.

Guilt and what we do with it, compels us to turn inward and push the world away. So I held to the more inviting feminine form for a couple of reasons. Females have a tendency to be far more inviting and intimate than the male counterpart. Her eyes are deep, rich, and powerful and look right into you. Not past you. Not around you. They beg us to come closer and leave us with a powerful impression from which we cannot escape. The crazy thing about eyes is that they never lie. The bricks in the picture represent the walls that we build to try and hide behind. The words invite you to see life through a particular lens.

Life bombards us with feelings of guilt that shape our motivations and actions.

Whether we react to how guilt speaks to us in fear or whether we choose to learn from it, we are all motivated Through the Eyes of Guilt.

Through the Eyes of Guilt

Motivation of Life "THROUGH the EYES of GUILT---- our morality defines our mortality and our mortality defines our morality

ALVIN EPP

BALBOA.
PRESS
A DIVISION OF HAY HOUSE

Balboa Press books may be ordered through booksellers or by contacting:

Balboa Press
A Division of Hay House
1663 Liberty Drive
Bloomington, IN 47403
www.balboapress.com
1 (877) 407-4847

Book cover photo illustration credit. Craig Minielly, Aura
Photographics. www.auraphotographics.com
Book jacket design credit Yasmeen Wedel, YW
Design Studio. www.ywdesignstudio.com
Chapter Icon credit, Sylvain Bissonette, Photo credit Samantha Zaharia

Printed in the United States of America.

ISBN: 978-1-4525-2055-1 (sc)
ISBN: 978-1-4525-2057-5 (hc)
ISBN: 978-1-4525-2056-8 (e)

Balboa Press rev. date: 9/19/2014

CONTENTS

CHAPTER 1

The Radio Host and the Interview

I was listening to the radio one day, and the host made a comment that caught my attention. The comment wasn't unusual because many people throughout time have said it before. The comment caught my attention because the way it was framed begged me to listen with a curiosity about how someone might respond.

The radio host was interviewing an author who had just finished writing a book about the mother heart of God. They were discussing the nature of God and how "he" is portrayed. Even right there, there was the connotation that God is male. I think most people are okay with the idea of God being a male-oriented supreme being, but is there much more to God, presuming we believe God exists, than just focusing on whether God is a male or a female entity?

The gist of the conversation was about why bad things happen to good people and why good things happen to bad people. The host finally asked, "Why would this apparent God of love allow bad things to happen in this world?" Over the years, the question has been asked many times—and many answers have been solicited—as we've searched for the answer.

Before I go on, maybe the question begs a few more questions. Why would a God of love allow all this bad to happen? Maybe the question has to do with our curious, probing minds needing an explanation for why we do what we do and what we are doing here on this planet anyway.

Many sects of religious orders define God's role in our human existence. In biblical narrative, the Old Testament characterized God as a judging deity. If you step out of line, God will take you down. He was a very dominant, male-focused warrior-type deity. The Supreme Deity was not to be messed with.

A shift occurred in the New Testament when Jesus showed up and redefined God. Jesus or Jeshua was much more maternal in his nature and demonstrated the character and nature of God. In his claims and life, Jesus was far closer to the Mother Nature characterization of God.

Interestingly enough, some of our major religions stem from the same Abrahamic father and can be traced back thousands of years. Mosaic Law—not the Ten Commandments—evolved into a list of rules that shouldn't be broken. If they were broken, serious consequences occurred to the perpetrator or perpetrators. By the time Jesus showed up on the scene, the "list of rules" was too onerous and complicated for people to even know where they stood with God. The system of the day supported the upper religious leaders to determine and define what was acceptable and what was deemed "right." If not, the warrior God would destroy them. Control was the dominant force for determining how people were kept in check.

Fear works wonders in keeping people in line, and religions are very skilled at creating dynamics like this. It works because humans have egos, and the ego lives in a separate state of existence in the human body. The ego is designed for self-preservation. The ego will do whatever is necessary to protect what it believes is in the best interest of the self. With this as the human condition, it is a small step—with several evolving movements—to go from innocence to appeasing guilt.

This guilt extends to the community and beyond. Why is that? How does that work? Why would humans have the pressing idea that guilt is part of our human makeup? Does guilt play a role in life? If so, does it serve us or do we serve it?

Back to my original question, if God is seen as a loving God, why do we abuse and misuse each other so often for our own gain? We have a will within us. This will says we have the freedom and capacity to be kind and forgiving and/or harsh and judgmental often within the same thought. I'm not necessarily referring to those events on the other side of the world or the major ones that capture our attention on a grander scale, such as mass murderers, dictators, and extremist groups that thrive on violence to satisfy their beliefs and values. I'm going to focus on everyday life where each one of us has to resolve how guilt fits into our human experience.

Why does a loving God allow all the horrible events of life to occur? Why couldn't God—if he exists—wave a magic wand to take out those bad dudes and make it all better? Wouldn't our world be better if God singled out those who commit these crimes? What if a guilty judgment could be exercised and the innocent knew the verdict was justified and could carry on as if nothing happened? The innocent? How quickly do we judge things—no matter how grand or insignificant the thoughts or actions might be? We like to be right in our assessments of whatever is brought to our thought processes. Our beliefs and values motivate us to come to conclusions that often make us the judge and jury and all too often the executioner as well.

The guest on this particular radio show was commenting on the nature of God's forgiveness and how far this forgiveness reaches. The comment was made that this loving God could forgive a serial killer or a mass murderer. If forgiveness is valid at every level imaginable, then everyone has the potential to be completely forgiven. The next thing the host said caught my attention. He didn't think or believe that the crimes committed by these individuals were forgivable. There appeared to be a line that determined forgivable actions and unforgivable actions. Society does it, but more importantly, individuals have something inside of us that calls the shots to determine what is and what is not forgivable.

Not forgivable! By whose criteria? If we say that an ethical and moral compass measures the human journey, where does the line get crossed—and who determines the line? It may sound easy to define and determine the outcome of the actions and behaviors of a serial killer or extreme actions of an individual or individuals whose behaviors and actions contradict our cultural moral code. So, how do we satisfy our own guilt when we bet on our perspective of guilt and judgment through the lens of the ego? Is the ego trustworthy?

CHAPTER 2

Guilt and Ego:
What Do You Mean?

What happens when we remove the apparent obvious crimes in life and digest our everyday world where we are often motivated by the ego? Is it possible to put down the idea of judgment and its desire to satisfy our self-preservation? Judgment presumes guilt. Guilt about what? If we need guilt to satisfy the ego, what do we gain from using guilt to journey through life? Does God—or a godlike deity—become the target of our guilt? Maybe by placing the guilt on God, we can appease the ego and carry on with our self-preserving judgments. Does guilt actually assist us in finding out how and why we are here?

Before I go any further, it's important to define the ego and my ideas about guilt. We create constructs around what we understand the ego/mind/consciousness/spirit to be. The ego is who we think we are—except there is so much more going on in our lives than what we can observe, demonstrate, or understand with the human senses. The ego has to remain in the realm of human existence because the body it resides in limits it. What is this self that we create to help us maneuver through life?

Ego is often used to mean the self. It defines us. Religious context defines the ego in relation to the soul. In religious teachings, the ego is characteristic of living beings with a higher level of consciousness, which is commonly understood to mean the "spirit." It is a form of recognition for us. What people believe about themselves is driven by the ego's interpretation of the self.

I use the word *ego* to identify who we are as human beings. When we show up on this planet, that is all there is. In other words, whatever happens here has to be understood through the ego's frame of reference.

Guilt is defined as an emotion that occurs when people believe they have violated a moral standard they believe in. It comes across as a moral judgment that the individual is blameworthy of something. Where our conscience can impose blame, it will punish. In order for our conscience to place judgment, it must hold to the idea that guilt is always before us. Being guilty presumes that we have failed a moral obligation to something or someone.

These two definitions should give you some level of context for how I define ego and guilt.

In the Old Testament, Genesis tells us that the two original humans had a perfect relationship with God. This ideal relationship had the dynamics of no shame or guilt and everything in its perfect form; at least, that is how the narration is presented. The idea of original sin and guilt was woven into the story of creation through deceptive means, and the fall of man became a permanent fixture of life. This new world order brought a whole new set of rules.

Apparently, there was no need for rules prior to this human fall from perfection. Now that the human condition had turned away from perfection, something else had to replace how life was lived. If the first couple hadn't messed up, would we all be in utopia on earth? I don't think so. I don't think that the story of the fall of mankind as we often interpret it represents how the human experience was to be fully embraced.

What is it about our human experience that pushes and pulls us in ways that boggle the mind? If the ego is designed for self-preservation—and it only knows what the senses offer—it makes sense that selfish behavior would be overwhelmingly rampant. It has to be. Self-preservation demands that "I" am looked out for first. We will do deeds along the way that demonstrate things that are fueled or motivated by our individual spiritual dispositions, but the ego demands full allegiance. What is our task here on earth? What is our journey? When we breathe our last breath, what will we understand about life and our experiences here?

It could very well be that the dynamic of the ego and all of its frailties actually creates the perfect environments for us. Something so amazing in what is our true self, in how it is that the spirit grows.

What is the journey all about? Are we here to go through a list of experiences, stay safe, and get out unscathed—or minimally scarred? What does this journey reveal to us about how we find the way home?

In this space of being human, the ego is driven to preserve and defend itself at its own expense. It will take out anyone and anything to accomplish its belief that this is all there is to existence. If someone or something threatens it, it will fight back. The ego will use fear, guilt, shame, blame, accusations, and other mechanisms to excuse its actions. The ego cannot stand that a spiritual dynamic wants to change its selfish nature. It has no qualms about sabotaging any attempt to come under submission.

In this battle, life goes to its core to determine why we are here and what we get to experience and grow through. In the intricate dance of the ego and spirit, another question needs to be asked. Who or what will help the spirit grow? How is that possible? We know within our conscience that we cannot escape the deepest parts of what makes us uniquely human. We call it the soul or the spirit within. We may attempt to numb this part, but the truth is that we cannot. We may try—and try hard the ego self will—but no matter what substance, thought process, structure, or product we use, we will always find the soul being defined by the very core of what sits in the seat of life.

The brilliance of this human experiment and experience in how we grow is quite impressive. We want to live in peace and happiness, and the ego will attempt to create the space for that to occur, but the ego will use fear as its primary motivator.

The ego believes that it can determine how peace and happiness exist by manipulating the space it fills.

Fear depends on guilt to measure life. Once this is set and entrenched, it is a small shift to continue that belief into who God is—and if he even exists. Fear captivates the ego and reinforces its belief that this journey of life is all there is. The ego thrives on fear and control. It satisfies the outer shell of existence. When conflict occurs between the ego human and the spirit, the war of life and identity wage nonstop battle. We may argue that there are two voices in our mind. One is called the ego, and the other is the spirit. We relate the conscience with that which identifies with spirit. What if we are more integrated and have these two voices within us, which orchestrates an amazing stage for individual growth, instead of looking at them as competing voices.

If the spirit wants something different, what might influence the direction and shape of how life is lived? The ego uses the excuse that it has to look good, and it will create structures to support its never-ending quest for self-preservation. When it is threatened, it will turn and attack.

I came up with a question while thinking about what drives the ethical and moral compass. Does our morality define our mortality or does our mortality define our morality? I tried to answer this question by using one against the other, but the more I looked at the question and the flipping capacity of the words, the more I realized that they both fit and blend into a much bigger picture. The statements and questions are intertwined and far more influential to life than we imagine.

This simple equation holds one of the central drivers for how we live our lives. We believe that an internal moral compass defines mortality. We believe that if we are morally upright, our mortality will be long and favorable. Subsequently, if we hold a belief that our longevity lies in our mortality—by our being morally pleasing—we will get to have a long life. Both can be beneficial, but both may be motivated more out of fear than we care to admit.

But who defines what is morally acceptable? We look for the line and/or acceptable behaviors that we believe will keep us from the wrath of an angry, judging deity. We believe this will ensure us long, prosperous lives. The same holds true when we hold the belief that mortality will not be compromised if we hold certain moral codes or ethics.

Is life guaranteed to be a long, mortal experience? Many people don't have that chance. Why do we cling to staying on this planet in human form anyway? I recently spoke with a seventy-five-year-old woman who wants to stay here and live until she is 120. I wonder why. What is the attraction here that holds this mortal soul with an end date predetermined by bodily functions (or the lack thereof)? Are mortal beings scared of something else? Since the ego dines on fear, it's not hard to see where not wanting to die is attractive for the ego.

Knowing that the ego is concerned with self-preservation, it's no wonder that the fight-or-flight instinct constantly bombards us. When we are pushed—or we believe we are being pushed—into a corner by circumstances that we feel we have no control over, we use the fight-or-flight instinct to escape the perceived danger.

The fight-or-flight instinct will feed off the ego's desire for self-preservation. And it will fight back. The fight is usually not physical. It may have physical consequences, but the primary determinant will be driven by the ego's insecure nature and what it can only experience by its very design, which is odd on some levels.

The human decision-making machine can create, procreate, solve problems, intricately determine human ailments, and have athletic capacity beyond compare. However, it can become unglued by a penetrating thought that nags at the conscience.

In fighting back, the ego wants to castrate and neutralize any idea that there is something beyond itself. That is why the ego loves the idea of guilt. Guilt is a neutralizer to its ongoing existence. The ego is great at keeping score. It has a way of only thinking linearly. From this standpoint, a determining set of criteria defines what is acceptable and what is not. In the absence of any other influences, this might make perfect sense. In a sports arena, we can measure and keep score of who wins a game, match, or a competition with a set of rules and points for a certain length of time. It is simple.

Religion often operates this way. In the absence of spiritual dynamics that confront the soul, we resort to a set of rules that need to be adhered to. This way, it is much easier to keep everyone on track and in a controlled measureable environment. Religion thrives in a system where those who embrace the doctrines are required to stay on track with the rules defined by those who interpret the doctrine.

There can be many benefits to order, continuity, and belief patterns that support a community. The ego can be very subtle in what it believes is right, and it can determine the punishment for those who step out of line. The ego will attempt to use guilt and fear to monitor the community, and it has a cheering section of likeminded individuals. This cheering section will feed off of itself. It will find ways to justify the framework in which the corporate ego operates. This is a recipe for entire communities—no matter the size—to be held under control.

CHAPTER 3

Sin and Guilt: Those Crazy Cousins

When the idea of sin as described in biblical narrative was introduced, it brought guilt, fear, and shame. As a result, people had to be punished for being guilty. It is where the ego thrives and lives in its finest state. As long as people can determine a guilty verdict, they need a judge and executioner to carry out the punishment. The punishment may vary, depending on the perceived nature of the crime, but it will find a fitting punishment.

Why do we like guilt so much? We place guilt on ourselves so that we can appease something we think is keeping score on our comings and goings in life. We love to place guilt on others so we can judge them as less than us. This way, we can justify our behavior and thoughts—believing we are right—and no one can tell us otherwise. As long as we continue to keep score in life, of ourselves and everyone else, we will judge with random recklessness and determined vengeance that we are right. Therein lays the ego's driven mandate to prove over and over again its ability to determine the outcome of life's experiences.

In religion, the ego thrives on this grid. The ego will recognize the idea that there is a Supreme Being or Deity, but it will not have anything to do with submission and servanthood unless there is something in it for the ego. This way, the ego can build a structure or platform to showcase how wonderfully it can perform. The performance commands a strict adherence to the script. Whoever gets to write the script also gets to direct the script and makes sure all the actors are complying with the ego's agenda.

Guilt will motivate us to do things we internally wrestle with. Peer pressure, family pressure, doctrinal beliefs, and religious beliefs push us toward a place that we don't want to go. Why do we buy into this behavior when we know the outcome will not serve us? Each of these influences can bring results that wreak havoc on the soul. The message is conflicting to our conscience, but we often lean into the persuasive power of the message and moment.

Family pressure will pull at the deepest parts of the soul because of "loyalty." We think that complying will eventually bring us what we need or truly want. So we hope. The usual result is a loss of self and a loss of what makes family relevant. The ego remains distorted by the contradictory nature of the choice. The internal conflict increases because guilt is reinforced as a means of staying in line.

A friend told me how this played out in his life. Late in life, Gary discovered that he had another sister. She was actually his half-sister because his dad had another child with another woman at the same time that Gary was born. After discovering this new family member, he explained how his parents and other family members responded. Some family members embraced the news with open arms and were welcoming. Others took a definitive stance, wanting to believe that this new family member didn't really exist. The discovery of the new family member brought up feelings of guilt and shame. Guilt demanded a reaction, and the response was denial. Memories of something that happened more than fifty years ago unraveled the ego's self-preserving, self-protecting stance.

Doctrinal beliefs, whether they are religious in nature or not, are close cousins to the peer pressure choices we make and play out in the same way as family pressures. The push to comply with the "community" magnifies and stretches internal conflicts.

When groups form by believing in a belief, cause, or theology, they manifest and give guidance to the greater group. This is okay because of the order and structure. We do well with structure, and it guides our decisions. However, in too many group dynamics, something evolves into decisions that contradict the individual. A select few take power and determine the roadmap. This dynamic creates the belief that it is in the best interest of the larger community to hold court. By exercising what they believe is best for every scenario, they create situations that appeal to the ego.

The ego created the idea to maintain control in the first place. Peer pressure motivates us to feel like we "fit" into the group. We want to belong, and we are often at odds within our conscience because we somehow know that something is amiss. Peer pressure pushed by doctrine will capture the ego's heartbeat. It will tell us to comply with the outer personality of who we are so we can fit in and be accepted.

The ego motivates people to believe they are doing the right thing. It also appeases the leader or leaders of the community. Community leaders hold power and will exercise that power to their own benefits.

The complexity becomes even more complicated when the community is religious in nature. In a religious construct, we must answer to the Supreme Being, a deity, someone, or something. The complexity goes one step further when the Supreme Being or deity has been defined by the human ego in how we should understand this deity—and to the standards that the ego can only accept. If this is challenged, the ego will fight to the end to dissuade and disprove an alternate viewpoint. Loss of control and being right is pretty much as difficult as it gets for the ego.

The ego thrives on guilt as its motivator, trying to convince us that the Supreme Deity is appeased by us staying in line and following the rules that are often prescriptive. Prescriptive rules are much easier to follow, keeping our scorecards up to date. We can keep tabs on each other and apply pressure to those who attempt to step out of line. If we follow the rules, no one will get hurt. This system works when there is an absence of something else that guides our decision-making.

Even in core, ego-driven structures, something deep inside us has to check and question the potential outcome. Without internal conviction and spiritual pull, we will be persuaded by the ego to go along with what is presented instead of listening to our internal subconscious voice that challenges it. This internal voice may scream loudly to the conscience, but most often, it very quietly nudges the spirit to look closer and consider other point of views and possible outcomes.

This is one aspect of the role that guilt manifests in our lives. Many examples exist in religious structures. People who use guilt to motivate their internal compasses often find themselves imposing self-deflating thoughts that push them away from life and trap them in a form of psychological mental health with varying levels of despair. The varying levels of despair caused by guilt shape behavior, and we end up living in contradiction to the soul.

We look good to the outside world, but our inner worlds remain silent to those around us—even though we are screaming that something isn't working. This conflicting space requires a resolution. We know it does because we send out and hear a constant message. *We want internal and external peace.*

What is peace? How do we keep it constant and continuous when life's constant challenges bombard our inner worlds?

CHAPTER 4

Women and Men:
We Are Different Indeed

I was watching a TV show about two couples who experienced marital breakdowns. The stories were similar in that the husbands felt ignored by their wives, and within a short period of time, they started looking for something to fill a need. The basic need of feeling wanted, acknowledged, and respected was the message being communicated to the viewer.

Both husbands looked outside for stimulation to satisfy an inner feeling of being alone or isolated. Resentment began, and an internal dialogue shaped the mind to take action, a basic human-driven desire. Both men ended up finding other willing participants to satisfy their urges and feelings of aliveness. Both had affairs; one was with just one woman, and the other had several one-night flings.

Each experience created the same initial euphoria, but once the men had completed their flings, they felt regret, shame, and disconnection. They found themselves further in isolation. The guilt they felt was overwhelming to their souls. Both felt as if they had pretty much committed the crime of the century. When the wives found out, they felt betrayed, abandoned, distrustful, and guilty for not being more aware of what was going on. The couples went through counseling and managed to solve their conflicts. The consequences were different for both; one couple divorced, and the other chose to stay together.

Allow me to take another look at what drives us to do the things we do and behave in the ways that have us dining on a full serving of guilt. Take the story above and consider what may have been happening internally, first for the men and than follow up with the women. Men think very linearly, and women tend to think much more in waves. Women are far more fluid in the process. Both make assumptions based upon how the ego wants life and relationships to work. This isn't always negative, but it just doesn't have the whole story behind the motivation of what the ego wants to occur.

Earlier, I mentioned that how morality defines our mortality and our mortality defines our morality. In this frame of reference, I explore what happens as life moves us along. Men have an internal mechanism that is driven by sexuality. His connection to life is hardwired into his sexual drive. If left unchecked, it will wreak havoc with his mind. His body will crave something that his soul cannot overcome. In the linear sexual focus, he will look for and find a way to satisfy his innate wish to feel alive.

The DNA of feeling alive is in this space of desire, lust, and want. Life will bring a series of constant challenges and problems to solve. Some of them never seem to end. It is there that men find the sexual drive to escape the pressure that constantly bombards their souls. Once they accept the driven desire and move into lust, which is primarily for the sake of feeling alive, the step toward the behavior and carrying out the deed becomes a fixation. In this space, the realm of aliveness is powerful and all consuming. He is driven to complete the deed of what the arousal offers.

This generates untold moments of pleasure and delight. It will also bring a lost sense of time in what the moment offers. The experience is as close to immortality as one can possibly experience. The complexity only shows up after the deed is done—when the male returns to a normal, conscious state. The body cannot handle the euphoria for more than a brief time. Afterward, the guilt becomes the focus within the ego. The need for self-preservation becomes evident and apparent. The soul is conflicted because there are multiple messages raging within.

How is it possible that something that feels so good and electric can also elicit such strong, conflicting feelings driven by the measuring rod we call guilt? What are we guilty of? Is this internal conflict the result of doing something inappropriate? Is it the result of using someone else for one's own gratification? The extreme of this kind of guilt plays out in the male psyche.

The drive to satisfy this feeling of euphoria culminates in a surge of guilt, which leads the perpetrator of the activity to remove the guilty feelings by destroying any evidence that occurred during the process. This removal of evidence is the ego's attempt to appease the mind of any wrongdoing. This will always backfire because the conscience cannot—and was not designed to—operate in this way. Thus, serial rapists and killers go to the extreme. They believe they have no option but to remove the cause of their human-driven desire. In these situations, there is a significant loss of moral conscience. The curse becomes increasingly active. The ego has been relentless in self-preserving, and blame must be afforded to an external focal point. The ego will not accept anything less. Guilt will rise to its zenith, and out of that, the soul will have to make a decision. The soul will generally buy into the ego's process of protection.

This may be an extreme example, but I believe the point is made that the ego will find a way to deflect any accountability. The degree does not matter. Yes, it will have different societal consequences, but the same motivating structure is underneath this exterior. We happen to be acceptable with what we define as lower-level guilt or acceptable guilt and its linkages to behavior. The dynamics are the same, and its root source follows the same pattern.

Is the same play occurring in women? I write from a male perspective, and I'm sure women will challenge my point of view. Women approach guilt in the previous examples through how the ego defines the situations. This ego's definition will feed off the idea that the woman is not good enough. It will drive the message home that an external grid primarily measures her self-image. This external grid is so entrenched that when relational challenges occur, the protective ego's measuring structure kicks into gear. The results will be complex.

Depending upon the woman's personality, she may experience guilt, feel like she failed to make the relationship work, or explain why she cannot trust. This trust-measuring grid is conflicted because her primary instinct is to trust. Trust is a gift to the human experience. The very design of her internal structure is to shape, build, and develop trust. The tragedy of life is in the undoing of this gift. The bigger tragedy is when trust is conflicted by contradictory messages. The messages will most likely come from the experiences that relationships offer.

Women are more fluid—as if in a wave in their approaches to relationships and sexuality. This dynamic is motivated through the lens of trust. When that link is distorted, the ego will find a way to self-protect and create barriers so that the approach and layering of trust will now be defined by ego-driven methods. There is wisdom in being cautious in how trust is manifested, but when the ego is determining the lay of the land, guilt will be the fuel for how she behaves.

The tragedy will be that women will send mixed signals about how they act and who they really are. Men will attempt to interpret what they see and are attracted to, and they will hear another message underneath. This is where guilt finds its way and creates a conflicted world.

Where men think linearly and become messed up by guilt after the fact, women will experience guilt in waves. These waves are internal; it's a long, drawn-out processes. The deep well of trust that women are capable of holding is also the same well that guilt will draw from and attempt to keep the woman in uncertainty. As long as a woman can be kept in the "come close, go away" messaging center, she will be plagued by guilt equal to or even more than her male counterpart.

In the movie, *Hall Pass*, the two male characters were given hall passes by their wives. The wives went on a separate vacation, and the two buddies had the freedom to chase skirts. The reason they were given the hall pass in the first place was because they were constantly looking at other women while they were with their wives. The wives were annoyed, but they decided to put the cards on the table to see how serious their partners were about what they thought they wanted.

The two husbands, like most males, create the "grass-is-greener" scenario in their minds based upon the linear, internal sex drive. This freedom they were given created a confrontation of morals. As they pursued their female prey, they were faced with what would happen if something really did present itself. The illusion had everything lined up, but the closer they got to a willing partner, the more they became unglued by what the moment might actually entail. Their bumbling antics were comical to say the least. The brilliance of the director in how he used comedy to illustrate the bumbling nature of the male ego.

What was far more captivating in the movie was the dynamic that was occurring with the wives. Initially, they were reluctant to give their mates the hall passes, but they decided to trust their guys to do right. Maybe this was just an immature guy thing, and they could live with it.

The wives began to ask themselves if there was something wrong with them and why they weren't good enough to get affection. The wives discussed the arrangement, and one of them was uncertain about the deal and asks the other if it was a good idea to give them the hall passes. One of the wives was at the point of frustration and said she had lied about feeling intimate with her husband because she was creating scenarios in her mind where she wondered who he was thinking about while they were intimate. Her trust was already compromised and conflicted. The step to experiencing guilt came in waves. Her friend said that actions speak louder than we want to believe. She said, "It is our role as women to fake it from 10:00 p.m. till 6:00 a.m."

Guilt over relationship struggles will sabotage in order to self-protect. Later on in the movie, one of the wives was attracted to a baseball player and ended up spending the night with him. She actually follows through with her desires in that moment. The disconnect at home with her mate was captured by the attention of the good-looking younger male athlete.

Even though this movie was geared for a male audience, there were some telling scenes that explain how women embrace guilt. One in particular has one of the wives having an affair with the sports jock and afterward, she felt remorse beyond compare. Her emotions ran rampant and she didn't know how to handle the guilt. She told the jock that she could never be with him, and all her trust emotions were baring themselves. She couldn't separate the desires and act of intimacy with how it related to trust, connection, and commitment. In a woman's mind, they are all enmeshed and intertwined. The difficulty was with how her guilt would reveal itself after being unfaithful.

Guilt uses many symptoms to reinforce separation of self. The directors played it out well and stuck with the traditional role of men and the no-consequence stance of desire and lust. The portrayal of the two bumbling husbands was mostly in the illusion. The portrayal of the good-looking jock was part of the game men play.

When the wife told the jock that she made an error and she could never allow herself to be emotionally attached to him, his response was cavalier. He saw it as nothing more than a moment of pleasure with no conditions or consequences, perpetuating the notion that guys just brush these experiences off like drinking another cup of coffee. Her reaction was classic; she felt the brunt of the emotional disarray that the moment created.

Women are designed to trust, and when guilt shapes how trust will be measured, it uses their emotional triggers to weigh as heavily as possible the level of guilt to be manifested. For the two wives, the story appeared to demonstrate how—no matter what they did—guilt was going to set in motion events that conflicted with their soul.

Guilt keeps us in check, assists our moral compass, and keeps us from doing harm. Very true. The point I want to emphasize here is that we will act out in ways that conflict within ourselves because guilt is used to motivate us to comply with outside agendas and outward behavior that doesn't motivate us to grow.

Is our journey here to make it through school, get a job, raise a family, and find a retirement package that affords us a leisurely life till we breathe our last breath? Conflict without resolve will drive the vehicle of vengeance at breakneck speeds—with very little concern about the consequences. We focus a tremendous amount of energy on economy. We have started the journey with a limited view of what this journey is about. The stage for and our activity is okay, but it has limitations. The ego thrives in the driven nature of this worldview. It can perform at its best and keep the illusion going. This is what is at the core of where we begin to experience the dynamic between the ego's self and the spirit.

The spirit calls out for something well beyond the limitations the ego wishes to hold onto. Guilt pretends to protect the self, but the spirit is nudged to go in another direction. The ego believes in following the rules of what it thinks is right, but it often changes them to satisfy the conflicting agenda it holds. The irony is that it often puts forward a message and solution that goes against how life might want to teach us about our journey here. It loves to keep score in life.

It judges with its own insecure point of view. This judgment mindset has to prop up the ego and push down anything else to a level lower than where the ego believes it has been positioned. It does not matter where the ego is standing; it always believes it is positioned higher than that which it is judging. It operates from a position of limited information. It has no capacity to fully comprehend or understand the full picture of any given situation or human experience. In this limited capacity, judgment flourishes—and the ego vies for position.

CHAPTER 5

Judge and Jury

The ability to accurately judge requires full knowledge of past, present, and potential future outcomes. At best, we can assess the past and some current conditions. We say we need to judge situations and people and be responsible to judge the very things that we see in life. How many times have we judged something with very little understanding or grasp of what we are judging? We believe our judgment is superior to the one we judge. I would propose that we relinquish judgment. Let's no longer form judgment "by us" but rather allow judgment to come "through us." There is a subtle difference that has such a profound effect on the potential outcomes of that which we are judging.

This difference in how we see judgments changes the way life is viewed and lived. Our perspective changes to encompass a worldview where we lessen the ego's place in influencing our perspective and causes us to see a world of different possibilities. Why does this work? It works because there is a whole different dynamic occurring, which is influenced by a spiritual connection that shifts the ego—and desperately feels at odds.

If the ego is going to hold court on pretty much everything we see and experience in life, what does the spirit have to say to assist the soul in the shaping our journey while we are here on this planet? Something innate constantly reminds us that there is something beyond our limited human senses.

I discovered something about our human condition many years ago while working in drug and alcohol recovery. I was working with men who had come out of detox and were searching for how life was to be lived without the drugs that had influenced practically every decision they made. The constant in all of their decisions was to protect the ego because internal conflicts were constantly raging. The idea that some drug, choice, or behavior would alleviate the deep, internal voice that wouldn't leave and kept reminding them of something different.

Society has come up with several descriptors about people's behaviors and addictions and what we should do to reduce the harm to self or society. Our programs searched for the instigator to what creates the crime so that the perpetrator can acknowledge guilt. This guilt was supposed to make the perpetrator live and act differently. There can be success in the method, but I believe the story isn't complete.

Every guy I met with carried the same internal mechanism to find resolve. No matter how much each one attempted to numb the internal pain and gaping chasm of connection, they felt the same wave of conscious awareness of life and its mortal parameters. Killing the conscience was impossible. No matter how deep the angst, the conscience always came back and confronted the soul and the ego about its mortal constitution.

I marveled at how each man had to find resolve in his own soul and the process of allowing the fully conscious mind to consider how life was to be lived and what determined the moral/mortal code of conduct. To the degree the mortal soul was challenged, the moral code would define how to protect the mortal soul. The ego concocted ways to do what was necessary to ensure that the mortal condition overrode the moral choices. For the most part, it would do so at the expense of the morality side of how they lived. The guilt—and intense dynamic—wreaked havoc on the internal soul/spirit/ego relationship.

The men had life experiences that seemed extreme, but each one of us is defined by the same set of parameters of how life is experienced and why we are here. We all face the same conscious awareness and moral/mortality compass, and we cannot escape the internal resolve about why we are here and what this journey holds. This smorgasbord of human experience teaches us more about whom we are as a spirit being then we can ever imagine.

Where did guilt come from—and why is it so powerful? According to biblical text, the first two humans were in an apparent state of perfect harmony with their creator (God). No guilt, shame, or sense of anything would remove the perfect conditions in which they lived. The narrative said that they were allowed to have and do all that they wanted besides eating the fruit of the tree of knowledge of good and evil. Why would they not be allowed to understand knowledge of good and evil? What was the basis for the argument and rationale by some deity or potential deities that didn't want these humans to experience the idea of what good and evil meant and represented?

Was the idea that humanity should only be in a place of naive bliss and enjoy the human experience in a perpetual state of happiness? Was the goal of the human experiment by a God or multiple deities to have a spirit being dressed in a human frame with blissful experiences and limited understanding of who they really were? Was the apparent perfect state between man/woman and God enough to exist for the entire human race throughout the space we call time? Is the picture bigger than what we have been led to believe? Why would God want to limit the human experience to living in a perpetual garden—and for how long? What is it about the original sin that angered God and sent the humans into a world of chaos? Their life would consist of hard work, toil, and death. The trap, according to the narrative, was set by a dark entity, commonly known as Satan. This twist of the story opened the internal eyes of these humans, and they found themselves naked, shamed, isolated, and guilty.

Here's my question. Did the first two humans, according to the biblical narrative, even grasp what choice was? The choice to experience something that had consequences beyond their sheltered state of existence. If they lived in a state where the perils of life didn't exist, how would they know what the ability to choose between good and evil even held for them? We tell each other that we are accountable for that which we know. We give latitude for those who say they didn't know and were ignorant of the understanding of that which the situation applies. Was something different at the beginning of humanity? Did they live under a different set of human or spiritual dynamics than we have today?

I would suspect they did, considering thousands of years have passed since the narrative was first recorded. The traditional teaching tells us that God didn't want the first humans to eat from the tree of knowledge of good and evil. He wanted the humans (Adam and Eve) to live in the immaculate, perfect garden. God wanted, according to the narrative, to have the humans enjoy his company and live on this earth under a closed canopy. It would appear that this closed canopy included physical life and some variation of spiritual connection.

Why would God, in all his wisdom, put something such as this tree of knowledge of good and evil in the middle of the humans' home? It would seem that the idea of setting a trap would be trickery or cowardly, knowing that the one you are setting the trap for has no grasp of what the trap holds as a consequence. Ignorance of what the choice might behold is a sure bet on the bait being taken. The narrative is convincing in how Satan (the serpent) was characterized. The ability to persuade the humans of choosing to be as God is and the ability to know everything was intoxicating. The story is perfect. The plot is arranged with precision to put the heroes (Adam and Eve) in a position to take control of their destiny.

The human ego saw an opportunity for self-preservation and acted upon it. Upon doing so, again according to the narrative, they immediately were able to see the complexity of life with their internal eyes/spirit. They did understand good and evil, but what was the evil they did?

In the narrative, they disobeyed God by becoming aware of who they were and what they were capable of as humans. The design of the ego mixed into a soul with a spirit had to be well thought through by God (who fully understood what might occur). Was he trying to protect this creation from ever experiencing pain, loss, anger, resentment, suffering, or limitations of varying degrees? I wonder how long humanity would have existed in the original state of euphoria? At some point, would the experiment have just ended because it served little value over a set period of time?

Maybe God had something far greater in mind. Maybe the narrative—as many believe—was actually to give the listener a description of where life on the planet started and was designed to tell us how separation began. Maybe the point of the story was to identify the characters, why we are here in the first place, and how the ego in the human frame actually positions us to find the way home. Religious dogma, for the most part, views the narrative as man's falling away from God and sin entering the realm of humanity. According to the narrative, that selfish craving set everything in motion for the entire human race, and that one act meant that God would have to judge the wrongs of the world from then on. If God was going to judge the actions of mankind, what place did humanity have in judging? If God were a god of love, how would he determine the outcomes of any punishment? Does judgment become the marker of existence?

Our existence and experience on the planet is defined by many different personalities, cultures, and nationalities. Underneath all of these differences, there is a basic need. That need is to be connected to something beyond what we see, feel, taste, smell, and hear. But, if we are disconnected, how do we know—and what tells us we are disconnected? If God's original plan was to stay connected, was there another way he could have accomplished the goal? Was the idea of being separate and potentially disconnected a risk that had to be taken? How can I know that I have grown in life if I have no idea what the growth offers me?

When one looks deeper into the road map for humanity, in light of thousands of years of prior human stories and narratives, it would beg the question that there just may be a very thoughtful plan to allow for the separation of the human soul. We don't like feeling isolated or alone. The ego has a plan to keep us isolated because it can remain in a self-preserving mode, which it believes will protect us.

The good news is we are not just ego-driven machines that rely on the need to protect. We have a soul/spirit that contemplates the wide array of possibilities that life offers.

If God's overall plan of salvation—saving us from our own misery of dysfunction of attack, judgment, and death—is to get us back home, what was required from him? What might be required from us to get back home? It implies that we had a home prior to making this planet our home. This home has a finite existence for a body that has volumes of limitations beyond its ability to breathe and a heart to pump life. If the possibility exists that we came from an eternal home, while we are human, we draw on the complexities of what life offers. The ego and its self-preserving frame of reference, is challenged by the soul/spirit that goes far deeper into the possible reason for what a spiritual connection might look like.

Why are we here? If we are here with a start date and end date, what do we discover about life during the space in between? This allotted measure of time moves us through a series of experiences in which life, in a constant manner, brings us challenge after challenge. We attempt to position ourselves to minimize or avoid many of the challenges that come to us. The ego believes it has to protect us from complicated life entanglements. The ego sees the complication, determines an escape plan, and pursues the execution of the plan with great effort. The ego has a marvelous method of working within what it believes by choosing to counterattack the current challenge. That is how it will save the day. It matters not what the stage or set of circumstances are; the ego's first priority is self-preservation.

I want to make a distinction here between the outward stage of life where we take on a profession or career—and maybe even take our creative sides to new levels to where we are motivated by internal forces that beckon us to consider life differently. I want to focus on our internal response mechanisms that relate to what we take away with us after the journey ends.

The dialogue plagues the internal struggle between believing we are here in some human form forever and the reality that death of the body is on the agenda—and we cannot escape. The ego will push away and prolong the agony that it has to deal with. Its final demise is an end date for which it has no usefulness afterward. The ego is only capable of being productive in a limited fashion when it can see through a limited, defined lens.

The plan is quite brilliant when one considers the complexity of the physical human body. The ego that is housed in this human body and the spirit within recognizes that there is much more at stake, and the spirit will prod and nudge the soul to see life differently than what the ego believes is possible.

I could be the most optimistic person about what I want out of life and observe everything around me through the lens of possibilities—and yet still be at odds and isolated in the internal struggle of what life is all about. The wrestling of the soul and ego as it observes life, through our personalities, talents, and skills never stops determining who will be in charge or how life should be lived. The soul will consider the options of what the spirit part of us contemplates—while the ego will demand allegiance to its very directed agenda. The soul, the core of the self, observes life and will be challenged to stay loyal to what the ego defines as life. These life parameters are, for the most part, disguised as gifts and promise far more than what really is. This propping up of the soul to remain convinced that this is it is where the ego creates the illusion of what it believes, which makes up this life

The ego can only see through its limitations of what the human experience can offer. It may recognize other components of what life has to offer through spirit, but its first priority is to stay the course in defending its existence and why it believes it should remain in control of decisions and outcomes of what it believes will bring the preservation of the human being it resides in. The brilliance of the design of the ego in the human frame is how it creates what appears to be a near perfect space for the soul to interact in a battle between what the ego offers and what the spirit realm offers. When we come into this world of humanity, we are bombarded by the dulling of what the world offers. The overwhelming sensory attractions will create illusion after illusion to satisfy the ego's primary point of existence. If anything comes along and attempts to persuade the ego otherwise, it will fight back.

But there is a conundrum that awakens within us very quickly as life progresses from infancy to childhood and into maturity. We cannot escape this as it consciously reminds us that something else is at play in this journey. The spirit reminds the conscience that knowing the difference between right and wrong requires a new frame of reference from which to operate. This spirit influence gives the soul the platform to choose between right and wrong.

The choice of what we do with the experiences we have with others in the community requires resolve. When we primarily allow the ego to determine the resolve, it will almost always first consider what is best for the self—with very little regard for others. This resolve of life choices through the ego may smile on the outside, but it usually lives in fear on the inside and almost never wants to expose its weaknesses. It might consider exposing a potential weakness, but to acknowledge the human limitation is to regard itself as insufficient and needy. The ego by design counteracts any sign of weakness as an opportunity to attack and create the structure to place itself above the perceived weakness and take out anyone or anything that may challenge the position it holds.

The spirit looks at life and the constant challenges that life brings and observes from a very different reference point. What ensues is an internal dialogue where a choice must occur. In our state of separation from something external, such as the relationship between humanity and God, was described in the beginning of human existence when humanity discovered the idea of good and evil. We are capable of choosing that which is influenced by the spirit and that which the ego demands as allegiance to the self. The spirit is placed in a precarious position in whether it will go along with the ego's logic or if it will shift the process to something else that it knows has more than just a conditional outcome. The spirit will often shape the decision of the ego, but it will more often than not rely heavily on the voice of the ego to make sure that there isn't an undermining of the ego's strategy to keep it in charge and in control of all outcomes.

This structure appears to work for humanity to keep us in a place of self-direction, of which the focus on our existence is the be-all and end-all. Death has little value to the ego and the spirit. They know that something else is at stake, but they don't know what to do to adjust the ego's preserving mindset. As long as the ego remains in control, the spirit will find itself with conflicting messages. The spirit will be influenced by an ego that keeps telling the spirit that this is it. This life is it; you better ensure that you are front and center on the stage.

The consistency of the ego is brilliant. You have to give the design of the ego credit for developing a unique structure from which to challenge the spirit and for creating a continuous platform from which to determine how the journey of life will play out.

Without any external influencing definers, the self with a spirit and an ego will go through life with expectations that can never be resolved. The illusion the ego creates will push harder and harder until the spirit within comes to a tipping point. The internal questions begin to challenge the status quo of what life means—and how it's supposed to end—and the apple cart of life begins to wobble. This process may be short, it may last years, or it may last a lifetime, depending on personality, determination, disposition to life around them, or how far a person has gone down the road to self-destruction. These determinants will influence the road to a mortal end date.

It is in this space that fear plays itself out in ways that catch us by surprise. This fear goes back to the beginning of human time (at least as described in biblical terms) to when Adam and Eve discovered they were separate from God. Fear pushed the envelope to the point where guilt was free to roam with unimpeded license.

Guilt and fear will feed off each other as hungry vultures feed on their prey. This particular prey for fear and guilt is the human soul. As fear embeds itself, guilt will grow; once the roots are firmly established, the soul will be drawn into judgment. It is in the guilt-fear-judgment recipe that humanity thrives—as long as the ego gets to remain in charge of how the soul believes it exists.

Even though the spirit is conflicted, it will go along with much of what the ego feeds off of. Out of separation, the digesting of fear, guilt, and judgment will demand an execution of the guilty party. The guilty party, according to the ego, is the soul. The irony is that the ego will go to great lengths to protect the soul; in full contradiction, it will also go to great lengths to punish the soul. Go figure. We are fully aware of wanting to be protective of ourselves and keeping ourselves out of harm's way. However, we will dive into the well of guilt and fear to allow these hungry ego-driven vultures to create a roadmap that keeps us in a state of separation and isolation.

The twist of this state is that the spirit within resides in a conflicting human house. The trap has been set, and the spirit—in its isolated state—will remain uncertain about the outcome of what life is about. One might argue that they are fine, they have life figured out, and the journey is okay as is— thank you very much. For the ego, this stance is perfect. It will never have to ponder the journey beyond the human mortal time-limited experience. It stands to reason why humans are convinced that we can find the fountain of youth. We are bombarded by illusions where we can have it all and that we will never have to face the Grim Reaper.

CHAPTER 6

Road Trip and
Roadside Attractions

You may be wondering where I am going and whether I am
on track with where I started this writing. How did I get to
bleeding the ego and its revealing agenda and the connection to
a radio host talking about God who was holding a measure of
judgment over a person because the actions of that person were
never worthy of forgiveness. Does the idea of guilt only carry
a limited array of possibilities? Does it only have the markings
of a weak soul that is incapable of making good choices?

The ego would love more than anything to believe that guilt
is nothing more than a manmade idea that can be overcome
by ingesting a drug, narcotic, or even the damning judgment
of another by putting others in a place of contempt. This act
of distraction becomes a desperate plea for the soul to feel
completely at a loss about what to do. The spirit may beg for
reprieve, but the ego will overrule and go the extra mile to

destroy what may look like an attack. The twisted nature of the ego will feed off corrupting measures because its source of existence resides in separation and isolation.

There is much written about spiritual warfare and whether demonic influence, satanic influence, or some other form of dark entity feeds off the human spirit while it is under the control of the ego self. This manifestation of spiritual conflict has confounded humanity for as long as we have explored its possible existence. I have been in situations where things manifested that were beyond explanation, yet I felt something more powerful than I was able to comprehend. The difficulty is that there is no logical explanation to the feeling.

Ego thrives in the human frame of how it defines logic. It may even be skewed logic, but nonetheless, the logic the ego holds, carries, or believes and demands its own evidence to support its demand for allegiance.

You might be asking how I went from guilt to introducing demons, dark entities, and weird spiritual experiences that can't be explained. Humor me as long as I have you reading these pages. My thought process may be more like a road trip where we get to stop at any roadside attraction and not just focus on getting to the destination. In some books, I read the first chapters, and when I want a succinct answer to the question posed, I read the last page where all is resolved. Then I can smile and carry on. However, life somehow doesn't work like that. It can never be compared to a movie or a book. I love a song by Supertramp; the lyrics go something like this: *The actors and jesters are here. The stage is in darkness and clear. We're raising the curtain, and no one's quite certain whose play it is.*

These lines beg the listener to contemplate life. We put on our costumes, put up our props, and wonder where they will take us. The illusion the ego creates is to keep us in costume, propped up so that we can avoid facing the mortal masks we wear. Theater, movies, and music are fabulous mediums to convey messages about life. There are limits in their structures, but they give us glimpses into humanity and call out to us to see life in a variety of ways.

I love to watch movies or listen to songs that go after the questions of life. They often convey more questions than answers. This is one of my purposes in writing. I want the reader to explore the questions of life and search beyond what we see with our eyes. I think our spirit longs to find attachment in order to move from separation to connection within the soul. You may or may not agree with where my reasoning comes from and why I believe it holds value, but humor me and contemplate what might just be a discovery of the journey home.

There is something in the spirit that calls for and continuously longs for the "truth" without illusions or props. No flags will fly that claim immunity from being accountable. No pointing fingers attempt to claim innocence. When one comes to the place where all bets are off, a shift occurs within the spirit—and everything changes.

I've watched many crime-related TV shows. The police and detective shows always carry the same plot. In the first few minutes, we witness a crime. The authorities show up and begin the process of discovering what happened, why it happened, and how it happened. They eventually discover the perpetrator. The questions of motivation, association, conflict, and myriad agendas are explored. The plot thickens, and we know when the criminal will be found out because the fourth set of commercials have come and gone. After forty-five minutes of reel time, we are just about there. The overriding theme of the script is to discover the "truth." In *Liar Liar*, Jim Carrey said, "And the truth shall set you free."

The funny thing is we all think we know the truth. We just have difficulty defining what is true. We will argue for what we believe is true and defend our positions because we make "truth" through an ego-understood measuring stick. The ego usually creates a framework that relegates the idea of truth to a human-defined list made up by its own rules of logic. This truth demands evidence—just like the police shows that require hard evidence to solve the crime. The ego, because of its limitations, will use hard evidence to determine whether something is to be believed or not. It can be argued that knowing the difference between what is true and what is false is good. In a lot of human interaction, this is true. We constantly make decisions based on whether we believe something is true or false.

In the midst of my rabbit trail around the ego and truth, I still want to keep in mind the idea of the role of guilt and how it motivates us in relation to what is at the core of our being and our existence on this planet. The quest for what is true is as complex as when we ask why we are here and what this journey is about.

Somewhere in the recesses of the soul, we press to know what is true. Just as the detective shows illustrate the need to bring closure to a crime, we want to have closure to our existence. The shows we watch will find the guilty party within that one-hour window. Humans need closure. We would be mortified if the crime show left us hanging, without knowing who committed the crime. The ego-driven agenda acts the same way. When we see crimes, wrongs, and perceived inequities, the ego demands that justice is served. The punishment has to fit the crime. We have this pressing need to judge and punish so we can feel closure.

What would happen if we were limited in determining what we believed were the facts? The ego isn't convinced that it is limited in knowing everything. We don't do well when we are told we are wrong. The difficult, sensitive nature of the ego will lash out if it senses an attack. The attack can have several layers of expression and reaction.

One of the common reactions is to withdraw and use self-hatred to deal with the attack. The ego quickly transitions into self-preservation and creates a protective bubble so that the pain is rendered ineffective. At least that's what the ego believes will occur. When we are exposed, vulnerable, or threatened, we pull inward and look for a defense to counter those feelings. The difficulty is that the opposite occurs. Self-protection changes to self-hatred and becomes fuel that separates the ego and the spirit.

The wedge grows until the roots take hold in the most fertile soil of the human soul. The ego locks onto whatever happens once the self-hatred feeds the ego enough ammunition to lash out, but it believes it is serving the soul appropriately. Internal conflict at this level never ends. It might be tamed for a few moments, but the minute there is potential conflict or uncertainty, the ego will bring out a dagger and place it deep into whatever is in its way. The action can be specific or random, but the "other" is never guilty. The ego—along with a developed self-hatred suitcase full of blame and resentment—will attack so that it can reside in the place where the mortal soul believes that a guilty verdict, punishable through pain, will ease the conscience and absolve the soul of the certainty of its mortal existence. Once the soul has been determined guilty, a verdict must be handed down—and the execution of the guilty verdict must be exercised.

The madness of this recurring nightmare for the soul has bothered mankind as long as we have existed on this planet. The conflict within is more agitating for the soul than any physical ailment. I'm not cheering for or endorsing physical limitations by intention or choice. Physical pain happens for a variety of reasons. The pain within the soul is different; we have to process our response to life through the soul, spirit, and ego.

My Friend's Experience

I had a friend whose IQ scores were off the charts. He found school easy, and good grades were easy to achieve. Figuring out the answers was simple. His difficulty was in creating relationships that were active and fluid.

Giving and receiving love, life, and energy was far more complex and challenging to him. This complexity within relationships didn't fit his thinking. If knowing information and getting good grades was easy, why wouldn't his relationships work the same way? Relationships demand a lot. They are at the core of how we live. Building, growing, and developing relationships with others reveals everything about what motivates us.

Some relationships last a lifetime, others find a place for a season, and some end because they've finished their moment of interaction. Not all relationships are designed to be happy-go-lucky friendships. Some are actually designed to push us and move us through life in ways that have us grinding our teeth and grimacing. We don't like those relationships. We think they are out to trip us up.

Most often, connections show up in our lives to teach us about ourselves. We say we attract what we think and dwell upon. I wonder if there is more to it than just positioning ourselves to attract the nice things in life. If that was the case, maybe we could just rub the genie in the bottle—and voila— our wishes would come out well before the gremlins of life show up. I wonder if the people we encounter with different worldviews really have a lot more to teach us.

My friend wanted desperately to be accepted amongst his peers; he would do anything to fit in. He got caught up in using narcotics to feel connected and believed that it was the way in. It was ironic that someone with such intelligence would be trapped into a world that would spiral into self-hatred.

I got a call that he was in intensive care at the hospital. He had overdosed and was unconscious for several hours. By the time he was found, the circulation in his leg had been cut off and had swelled to three times what was normal. When I finally got to the hospital, his leg was in traction and cut open so the swelling would go down. The sight of his leg cut open and the tragedy of what the overdose caused was not pretty, and he was in a significant amount of physical pain.

I began to ask him what happened and how he ended up in the hospital with such significant injuries. He said he craved his drug of choice and ended up in a back alley. He shot up in a stairwell. He wasn't quite sure how many hours he was unconscious, but it was long enough to cut off the circulation in his leg to the point that he was near amputation. Someone found him, and he was rushed to the hospital. He was in agony. I finally asked what hurt more—the pain in his leg or the pain that was floating through his soul?

Without hesitation, he pointed to his head and said, "Up here, the pain is far worse than in my leg."

I stared into his eyes, looked deep into his soul, and glanced at his leg. It had been cut open from his knee to his ankle to release the poison that had accumulated from a prolonged lack of circulation. I tried to comprehend the physical pain he was experiencing. I looked back onto his eyes and searched for the layers of life experiences that had brought him to this place of self-hatred. The pain in his words and eyes reflected a tortured soul. He was conflicted by the ego's attempt to protect him and a soul/spirit that was trying to live differently. The difficulty and complexity of human craving—and the wish to feel connected—is far more complex than just making choices that will make everything better. He eventually detoxed from the drugs, and his leg healed, but he couldn't heal the inner turmoil that motivated him to live differently.

Not long after that, I got a call from a minister who trying to help my friend. He was contemplating suicide as an answer to what he was agonizing over. When I got to the pastor's office, my friend was lamenting everything life was throwing at him. The list of resentments and anger over perceived wrongs was growing with every breath. The angst and anguish compounded his internal conflict to such a degree that he was ready to explode. His whole personality began to shift in ways that would unsettle anyone. By the time he finished his commentary, he was ready to end the journey so that he wouldn't feel the pain anymore. The pain was too great to carry, and the idea of suicide, so he thought, was the answer.

I asked him how he wanted to end his journey. I wanted to know how far along he was in planning his exit—and where we could expect to find him. Did his plans have enough details that we would know what to expect? I knew that his thought process was thorough (given his high IQ). His personality also displayed a characteristic nature and understanding toward cause and effect and how that might shape the desired outcome.

He said he didn't have a plan or a specific place he was going to terminate his life.

What became very apparent was his frustration to be able to handle the inner conflict that resided in the space where the ego, who's DNA will drive the agenda for survival even to the point of death, and the soul who knows that life is far more intricately woven for something else besides showing up on this planet and just experiencing humanity with little or no purpose.

This conflict had been nagging at him for such a long time that he believed there was no alternative to suicide. The overwhelming feelings that were spiraling out of control were too much to bear. At least, that was how he felt. When we finally got around to what was really happening, he relaxed and talked about the anger, hurt, helplessness that surrounded his soul. Lashing out at everyone was the coping mechanism that his ego thrived on and used to keep itself in charge.

This story is an example of what plays out within each of us. My friend's journey reflected an image of what goes on in each of us. We experience these same core dynamics in different ways, but because our personalities are so varied, we learn to manage them with a unique individual lens. We cope with them accordingly. The thing I find consistent among humans is that we consistently cannot escape the constant push-pull that occurs within.

This push-pull is at the core of our choices, beliefs, and values. For the most part, they define what we think will make life work for us. Guilt plays itself out in very subtle ways. We are told and believe that guilt will motivate us to do what is right or fix a wrong. Being guilty of an infraction calls us to make amends for a behavior or action that offends another. This type of guilty verdict is measurable by our choices.

When I offend someone, I know it. When I know I have offended someone, I measure the outcome by apologizing and allowing the division or offense to dissipate. The outer offenses or actions that create division or separation are merely reflections of how we use guilt in the inner dialogue of our motivations.

My friend compiled a list of people he believed had wronged him, but the people on his list probably didn't even realize they were the target of his anger and resentment. How often do we target our internal messaging toward someone or something that has no grasp of what is being stirred? If we fully embrace

the trajectory of judgment by using anger and resentment—
because somewhere in the recess of our thinking process, we
interpreted the message as attack to the ego self—the attack
will always play out in ways that create circumstances that are
counterintuitive to the spirit.

CHAPTER 8

Theology and Mental Health

My quest is to unfold the area of life that feeds off of guilt in an inward way. The inner tug by the ego wants to judge and not be accountable. In much religious teaching, the emphasis is on submission to a deity. This deity expects full allegiance to what is believed to be the path to eternal bliss. Even if one doesn't believe in a deity that observes every action and thought we have, the same human parameters need to be resolved. Whether you are a follower of religious teaching and hold the dogma of its teaching where one believes there will be an eternal reward or hold the view that nothing exists beyond the blood flowing into our heart and breathing air moment by moment with no eternal existence, everybody still gets to have the same experience. We all die. The mortal experience will come to an end. I hold the belief that there is life beyond this journey. Many don't, but I wonder if that really holds true when the time that life offers comes to an end. I wonder if the question about the possibilities of life beyond the human experience in how we are hardwired hits harder as the soul contemplates the deeper side of why we exist.

Are there definitive answers to what I am probing and trying to frame as something that hits at the very core of why we are here and what we are supposed to achieve or take with us once we are done? To be definitive means that there is certainty. Maybe my idea of something that is definable by a certain set of parameters is conjecture and nothing more than a belief in something that is made up in our madness about what defines life and our longing for some sort of certainty beyond this world.

The teachings of certain religious belief structures teach that God will be answered to. How we choose to spend our time and the actions we take will determine our positions in the hereafter. I won't dwell on a variety of religious thinking, but I refer to the realm of evangelical Christian theology. The common theme among evangelicals is that we were created in God's image—and the hope of eternal glory rests in a personal connection with God. How that all plays out is as varied as there are denominations and theological constructs that support unique beliefs and values for each given denomination.

The interpretation of biblical narratives rests with the ideals and definitions of what any group determines the narrative to mean. The literalists determine that nothing can be deviated from the translation. The liberalists will go as far as they believe grace affords them to go. Somewhere in between, there is a host of theologies and practices in what is acceptable behavior and what is crossing the line. Crossing the line creates the unease of what might be a suitable punishment if there is a presumption of guilt for even thinking about stepping out of line. We will define what we believe "the Almighty" has decreed as "righteous living."

The influence of religious teaching and instruction permeates our culture. This can have positive effects upon society, and it can be detrimental. We do well with checks and balances, but there is more to it than that.

The difficulty is not in the pursuit of discovering God or believing in a deity that promises us an eternity beyond humanity, which is supposed to be filled with riches and rewards beyond compare. The challenge unfolds when the ego muddies the water of what the spirit hopes and wants us to discover.

We can say that we don't believe in any of this religious dogma or interpretation of what is or is not of God or whether God might even exist. We cannot escape what lies at the base of the human soul and begs for a resolve to the journey and how or why this life even matters.

No matter where one may travel or in the listening to our community voices, and or governments, care about our mental health. There is significant discussion about how we deal with mental health, the challenges the business world has with absenteeism, illness, changing staff, complex family dynamics, and the spiraling nature of depression. Where did all this come from? Governments spend a considerable amount of time and money figuring out how to reverse the trend of what mental health brings—or doesn't bring—to society.

Policies, programs, and resource allocation all play into an industry that has recently grown to become one of society's most complex challenges. We have been told to work hard, dream the dream, and achieve it all so we can have the luxury and comfort the ego craves. It knows nothing other than what we can offer. This tension is continuously rising and running a course until something in society snaps—unless we turn a corner and look at life through another lens.

Mental health professionals have an enormous task in identifying what motivates the human condition and understanding this human condition. The profession must also be able to diagnose chemical imbalances, physical conditions of varying degrees, and a host of varied thinking patterns with an attempt to at least manage some of the challenge with pharmaceutical drugs.

How did we get here? Where has this brought us? What happened along the way that life told us we can fix the ailment of our human condition and not have to face what our mortal life reminds us of? Separation was brilliant in that it created the perfect environment in which we are constantly in a state of tension between what the ego determines as life and what the spirit nudges us to consider about how life is to be lived. The ego has an interesting limitation in that it only knows how to protect and put on a good show.

The world is going through an evolution. What we thought were the rules have been dismantled, and we are facing a new set of measuring grids for how to see life. Will this new dynamic be our saving grace? Will it start with all the right intentions and energy—only to be fooled into an illusion of another kind? If we continue to let the ego run its attraction toward separation and isolation, we can be drawn into illusion quickly with the nature of how the ego defines existence. We are quick to embrace the latest fad or marketing gimmick based upon a quick fix to life's problems and frustrations. We want to believe that we are who the ego believes we are.

We confuse our personalities with whom the ego tells us we are. The ego will take our personalities and twist them just enough to create comparisons with other personalities. The idea is to reinforce the mad idea that you are nothing more than an amalgamation of body parts; if you don't control the space you're in, someone else will. Your personality is your unique signature of what gets you excited, the skills you have, and your capacity to understand life through your personal signature. The ego loves to box people into corners and put them under microscopes. It lives in a world of separation, fear, and isolation. The ego will use comparison to form judgment—and not see differences or honor the differences.

In writing this book, I spent a lot of time in coffee shops. The writing environment was perfect for meeting people. When asked what I was doing, I told them I was writing a book.

Most people asked, "What are you writing about?"

I would say, "I'm writing a book about life. The title is *Motivation in Life through the Eyes of Guilt: How Our Mortality*

Defines Our Morality and How Our Morality Defines Our Mortality.
By the time I finished giving out the title, I could tell their
minds were racing with thoughts and questions about guilt and
what it means in how they have dealt with it in their own lives.
The questions and comments about guilt created a stimulating
conversation.

The idea of guilt has a very quick thought process. We
all have experienced the nature of guilt. It is so central to life
and our journeys that we couldn't live without it—at least not
as long as the ego gets to determine how life will be lived.
The latter part of my title got the most curled reaction. There
was always a pause in considering the words and attempting
to digest what they meant considering how the words were
grouped together.

The next question was usually about the last part of the title.
Your mortality defines your morality and your morality defines
your mortality? One simple letter completely changes the entire
understanding of a word. Add the letter T to the middle of the
word morality, and the meaning goes to a whole other realm.
Remove the letter T, and it completely changes the meaning of
the word. Are the words moral and mortal of the same family?

Morality means to have proper behavior with intention.
Mortality means to have limited life expectancy. We are
reminded often of being in a mortal world. Every so often,
someone we know gets ill or dies. This reminder of the fragile
nature of life nudges us to live as morally as possible. We fear
the last of our breath and attempt to prolong the moment with
every resource we can muster. We engage a moral compass to

ensure that our existence will go on forever. The ego is framed with this logic and will construct life around the prolonging of our journey here. The difficulty it will create for the soul/spirit is that it will use the moral code of the human and twist it just enough because the mortal human with an ego in charge is based upon separation and fear.

It is here in my statement about our mortality defining our morality that the ego will influence what we think is morally acceptable. We know that good morals will keep us safer than not having good morals. The rub is when the ego distorts the moral code just enough to define the rules about what is morally acceptable. This is the space that plays out so delicately. We have that inner voice that gives us direction about life, and yet the ego will have constructed a paradigm about how the moral code should be lived—most often in the form of judgment of others.

This moral code often contradicts the ego and the soul/spirit. It will go along with the basic principal of what is morally acceptable until it is confronted by its own goalposts about what life pushes up against toward the owner of this ego. This face-to-face confrontation pushes back and creates an inner tug-of-war between the ego's idea of morality and mortality that without a transcendent perspective of life will usually result in the moral code being subjugated to the wishes of the mortal code. This will play out on many levels in life. It will often find fear as the motivator to hide, protect, and remain isolated from what might happen if someone finds out that there was a violation of the code. Who defined the code anyway? How did we know that there was a code that should be considered? Is there something far more engaging in life that is within each of us and needs to be drawn out of us?

What happens when we flip the sequence of words and look at them the other way? "Our morality defines our mortality." We hold a moral code because the ego believes it gets to have a long enduring life it believes it has been promised. We will embrace a moral code that holds us steady, and in doing so, we should be given the chance to live a long life.

The ego has no choice but to see life that way. Its very design is in this frame. It is here that the ego plays a subtle game again. When confronted by its own mortality, the moral code will shift to accommodate the ego's expectant life span. It does not want to die. It will engage all measures at its disposal to hold onto what it detests. Death is the ultimate slap in the face to an ego that sees life as all there is—and no one better get in its way.

The ego will draw upon its own resources that it was designed for and will bring out its primary weapon. The weapon is guilt. For once it has broken its own moral code; guilt will rise to the surface and start shooting. The ego will scream about how something caused this feeling of guilt, and the blame has to be placed somewhere. It definitely won't be placed on the originator of the one pulling the trigger, and it won't stand for the guilt to be faced inward and needing resolve.

Pull the trigger on guilt, and the rest will take care of itself. Guilt zeros in on the target, and once the target is focused upon, the accusation is made. An accusation quickly renders a judgment, and the judgment must have a verdict, which becomes a sentence. This sentence will require an execution. At that point, the trigger of guilt will have weaved its magic—and the execution will not go well.

Have you ever noticed yourself or watched someone whom when confronted will try to hide, minimize, or even deflect what looks like something that appears to be attached to guilt. The ego loves to accuse and turn inward to its own eyes of self-preservation.

The irony is that the execution of the judgment will have taken out the external target and systematically dismantled the inner moral code, creating a conflicting smorgasbord of turmoil. The mad idea that the ego believed it could protect the soul from harm only reinforced the struggle and impacted the mortal soul by creating conflict instead.

Does guilt cover every aspect of life while we make decisions about our experiences? We can live without guilt, can't we? If there is no concern about what happens after we finish out our time on earth, should guilt even enter the thought process or coerce us to adjust to the things in life that we have to make decisions about? Why does guilt even play a role in our world? What nudges us to consider a response that is based upon the inner workings of the conscience? Does conscience need closure and resolve? If so, why? And what is the relevance? No matter how hard we try to tell ourselves or position our belief systems to not have anything to do with guilt, we cannot escape the place within the soul that seeks resolve and why we are here on this planet. We will create as much structure as we can to defy the inner voice that begs for something far more empowering to assist us during the journey.

Guilt tells us that something has gone awry. Guilt checks our guts to see what we feel when an uneasy inner cringing occurs. Guilt can motivate us to right a wrong. Is guilt a neutral entity designed as a mechanism to keep us from causing harm to others? It's like when we attempt to shortchange a person. It's like when we are about to do something that may violate our moral ethics, and this feeling of guilt germinates. We feel the same way an addict feels when the craving for a drug begins to draw their attention.

This feeling of "feed forward" is built into the conscience as a tool to inform us that some action or behavior is about to force us into a moral decision we may or may not like. The time between when the senses pick up a feeling of guilt and the action that causes the guilt triggers something within the conscience. The soul and spirit operate from a different point of reference. The soul can easily be influenced by the ego's definition and learn skills and behaviors to deal with guilt. There is something inherent in all of us that we need to reconcile the disparity between what happens when we do something that pushes up against our conscience. It is here that the spirit confronts us about what we need to do to remedy the dilemma.

The biblical narrative says that mankind fell and found itself exposed to a world of sin. This sin created a division and separation from God. God became angry at his creation and banished them from his garden forever.

The conflict is always stirred by the ego's rationale that someone is less than; in order for the ego to survive, it must destroy the perceived enemy. Whether real or not, it will judge from a position of needing a verdict to satisfy the uneasy feeling of guilt. Is conflict real? Does it exist if we don't buy into the logic it holds? Would we judge the same way if conflict weren't in our hands?

Much has been written about conflict, but my introduction to the influence of how conflict permeates our world relates the madness of conflict to how guilt feeds off of conflict. Guilt is like fuel to a fire when a conflict of the ego's values rubs against someone else's perspective, behaviors, or actions.

We have very little difficulty bringing conflict to the forefront of any situation when we are in a place where very little resolve happens internally between the spirit and the ego. This drive for self-preservation by the ego will take a scenario of possible conflict, and if it feels threatened, it will either run or fight. The fight-or-flight instinct will retreat to self-defense and pulling away, using the victim's mentality as the rationale for its behavior. The fight-or-flight instinct will shoot down anything that appears to look like attack as fast as possible. The judgments will look slightly different in both cases, but the judgments will surface and become a verdict of guilt toward the other. The tragedy is that in both situations, the ego cannot escape the internal feelings of guilt that play perfectly into the equation.

It is about what happens within each of us as we face the complexity of life's challenges. Conflict is part of this journey.

From what we can tell, it started at the very beginning of human existence. Are we able to completely remove conflict from our existence? No, we cannot. Are we able to remove feelings of guilt from our existence? No, we cannot.

The list of human attributes that confront us is lengthy. This design is brilliant when you think about how we grow through the complex dynamics of human existence. Our unique personalities measure our existence by what we were given when we showed up on this planet. Our personalities filter what we believe our values should look like. Our varying perspectives on life are designed to allow us to be creative. This creative nature mixes with skills and talents to build communities. We don't do well in isolation. There are far more complementary layers of life that suit us well when we allow the spirit to engage the movement of life within the variations of our unique differences.

CHAPTER 9

Harmony in Tension

The world we know lives in tension. This tension is a positive aspect for how life is lived. I call it "harmony in tension." Is life always harmonious? Are we able to hold life in balance? We have heard lots about how to keep balance in life. Balancing life reminds me of a guy with a large pole walking on a tightrope. This image leaves me with the impression that as long as one remains focused, not much else can be involved for fear of distraction and certain death or crashing resulting in a large mass of personal injury.

I prefer the word harmony to balance because I think it better reflects what life holds for each of us. Harmony in the context of singing is something we all love to hear. The sound will soothe the soul, stir our emotions, and engage every fiber of our beings. There are scores of songs that use harmonies to create overarching scales of emotions. The songs can be written in the simplest manner, the lyrics can be as shallow or complex, and the singer may sound okay or great as a soloist, but adding harmony brings an entire new range of emotion for us.

My brothers sing in a barbershop quartet. I love to hear them perform and how they blend their voices in harmony. I was listening to them one time, and a lesson was driven home to me. Harmony is a more accurate word for how life plays out—at least in the way I see it.

I would watch the four of them singing in harmony, blending together, and one of them would step forward to sing a lead melody. The sound by the soloist was pleasing. What made it so pleasing were the harmonizing voices behind him that complemented the sound that he was bringing to the melody. The harmonizing was far more important than just a blending of voices to complement the soloist.

The value of harmony is that several parts make up the whole. This makeup is crucial for how life interacts within us. Think of it this way. Each of us has several layers of life happening simultaneously. We have family, work, leisure, and our community involvement. All of these competing and complementing interests push and pull in different ways, at different levels, and at different times.

We also have several layers of competing and complementing interests in what we want to focus on or achieve in life. Our personalities give us the clues for which areas of interest pique our attention. Some personalities lend well to managing structures defined by numbers, calculations, and systems. Others see all the colors in the rainbow and just have to paint, write, or finely hone the music within them. Some will be entrepreneurial and develop business and others will be health-care specialists. These variables create the mosaic of life. Our personalities create interactions with the varying skills and talents we all carry.

As we go through life, we connect with several layers of interests—often at the same time. We operate best by having a wealth of support to uphold us when we prioritize something we believe is important. I believe our world was not designed to be an either/or world.

As I listened to my brothers sing, it was fun to hear one of them step forward to sing solo. Their voices created a pleasant, distinct sound that was easy to listen to, but not one of the four could stay in the lead melody position for very long. It was taxing on them to have to sing with more energy and complexity as they sang solo. There came a point where they would back up, rejoin the group, and fall into the harmonized blended voices—and becoming almost one unified voice. This illustration shows that it serves us well to have a wealth of support for times when we need to step forward and show the world our gift to life. The picture of harmony has several layers of strength through the different sounds and talents of the singing voices. If one can sing tenor but not bass, the sound becomes limited by a certain projected sound. The support of the bass, alto, and baritone to the tenor makes the song mesmerizing to the soul.

When we embrace life through harmony, we give attention to the outer world and the inner world. We also find far more strength in our decisions and responses to the complexities of life. When conflicts occur or challenges of varying degrees push our buttons, we know that there will be an opportunity to respond, knowing that we have a very different set of supports to backstop our life journey.

Tension is important to how life is measured. Tension is pulling through force, the idea of stretching, or a form of applied stress. We don't like tension—at least not when it creates a negative feeling. We say we can feel the tension in the air when we see two people at odds or a disagreement in a group.

The clashing of values or ideas creates the stage for tension. This definition of tension finds its way back to how we respond to life. What recoils inside us when we feel this kind of tension? We run, find a place to hide, or enjoy the adrenaline rush that the tension brings. The ego will thrive on the rush of the tension if it's in the ego's interest. Internally, we flip back and forth. The idea that my way is the right way and the obvious error of the other person plays well into the ego's self-preserving mandate. This form of tension fuels judgment.

What if tension isn't a negative word. What if tension is exactly what is needed for us to live? What if tension is the catalyst that causes growth within us? The definition of tension by which we will be stretched and pulled is very much a strength of the spirit's way to achieve the goal of why we are here. Tension will draw us out of uncomfortable spaces. Tension never stops, and even when we grow through one level of tension, another will surface and pull us even further along the journey. The idea of tension is not to tire us—but to assist us. Tension is never meant to be reactionary or compulsive.

Allow me to illustrate. A guitar player is always listening to how his instrument sounds. A guitar has six strings, and each string plays a different sound. When each string is in its proper level of tension, the sound will harmonize and capture our attention like no other. Even the most tone-deaf person will hear when the strings are out of tune. The sound will just seem off. We will tune out the sound and want to run away.

The task of the musician is to continuously listen for the required level of tension to keep each string in tune. The ear will improve its ability to fine-tune the tension of the string as it practices hearing the sound. The musician will never be reactive or aggressive to what is needed. Watch musicians when they play guitar. They will always be listening to the sound of all the strings, and they will delicately tune the strings and keep them harmonizing with each other. They never ignore one just because the other five are in tune. It would drive a musician crazy because the sound would be agonizing.

The tension is the brilliance of the instrument. The musician skillfully keeps the tension aligned to the benefit of the listener. The point I want to emphasize is that the task is to attentively listen to what is happening to the strings in our lives so that we can make the adjustments that keep the sound through this tension alive, engaging, harmonizing, and pleasurable to be around.

These illustrations are meant to give us a perspective on how life works. The ego has an agenda and will want to just play solo. Even worse, it may believe it is making an amazing sound when most of the strings are so far out of tune that it makes a jarring noise rather than a symphony of blended sounds and voices. The ego believes it can sing every part of the harmony and still sing solo above it all. It will exhaust its energy to prove that it is capable of performing all the parts—only to discover that it will strain itself while pretending the illusion is wonderful. The song in the ego's frame will be the sound it believes the world wants to hear. The illusion continues, and the conflict within carries on with this mad idea. Excuse my odd sense of humor but, the idea that me, myself, and I, is what the ego thrives on. Reminds me of a movie made several years ago where the main character wrestles with split personalities to deal with years of continuous abuse. This rude and violent personality caused by delusional schizophrenia and narcissistic rage goes around retaliating against anyone who gets in his way, even harming those who didn't do anything to him. Isolation remains, and separation continues.

Tension in harmony keeps us from falling into the ego's trap of self-preservation. We actually work quite well with tension. It would appear that the brilliance of our existence here is experiencing this constant tension that reminds us when we need to adjust. The ego knows this, but it often uses reactionary measures instead of allowing the internal spirit's quiet voice to shape us and move us through life.

When we allow the spirit to negotiate the journey, everything changes. Even when we feel we have conquered some of the ego–driven agendas and know the source of our angst, we can get caught in a web of ego-fueled situations. Debates and conversations become arguments and conflict because something in the mix pushes the ego to react to invite judgment.

Welcome to a life filled with never-ending challenges to the human condition. I had one of these experiences lately. I was in a conversation, and the discussion turned to "either/ or and someone had to be right." I felt uneasy as the right or wrong thinking became the focus of the discussion—rather than a discussion about the complexity that the issue evoked.

The issue was emotional for the other person too. The reaction was far more intense than I anticipated. I thought I was just having a discussion. What I didn't anticipate was how emotionally charged this particular issue was going to be for my friend. I was more taken aback by how fast we react when our emotional trigger points get bumped. This reaction surprised me more than the person's actual point of view, but that is what makes the human existence so amazing and colorful.

We carry different perspectives and opinions, which is something to be celebrated. However, the issue, opinion, or point of view is not the concern. The deal will always be in how we react and how fast we react to the circumstances in front of us. In that particular situation, I had to catch myself to not get drawn into the messages being sent.

The ego is skillful in attacking, and it is a very small step for all of us to be captured and come up with our own attacks. The issue becomes irrelevant, and the ego's sole goal is to drive a wedge into the moment because it relies on its position of control to survive.

It was fascinating to step back and observe the interaction with my friend, I felt uncertain for a few moments. Should I shoot back, stop and think for a moment, or throw a nasty dart back to prove my point? I realized what was happening and stepped back. It was a brief moment and a short conversation, but I was reminded that an uneventful conversation can trigger a reaction when the ego feels attacked.

If we are unable to pick up the clues in the moment, it is as simple as flipping a switch to go into attack mode. This doesn't mean we don't debate with full-on emotion or become passive. The difference will be in how we demonstrate our actions and respond in the moment. When we are aware of what drives our inner responses, we are far more likely to bring our perspectives with full emotion—without attacking. Something in the spirit will redirect how we assess and respond. This approach will be received far differently. The ego won't have a chance to attack. The outcome will feel very different to those within range of the discussion.

Those who learn to see their spirit as a guiding vessel to how they live will see the world as a place of learning—a place to develop the inner soul.

CHAPTER 10

The Brilliance of
the Human Experience

Is there something else we need or require to assist us in finding our way home? Religious groups have a set of criteria that we must meet in order to get an eternal reward. Other spiritual orders see the universal energy force as giving us what we need to live through the journey here.

There is an emphasis in our world to consider meditation as part of the journey. What is it about meditation that pulls us toward it or repels us as a weak excuse for living life? Is there something to it that gives us a grid from which to live? Religious groups of all stripes have used meditation and/or some form of prayer to frame the spiritual life. Are all these groups meditating and praying to the same entity? Does meditation carry the same benefits regardless of the style of practice?

I have read many books on the subject of meditation. Many look at the connection of meditation to the inner self, the divine source, and the connection to some sort of universal energy. Does it matter to whom you meditate? Do we need to have a focus of our meditation—as in the form of a deity—or is enough to rely on ourselves to achieve the desires of what drives or motivates us. Do we need to answer to a god or deity? Is there something beyond the human ego that begs us to look deeper into life?

What we think or believe is important. What do we value—and why do we have this voice deep within us that begs for connection? A connection to the ego nature—as long as the spirit goes along with being nice—should get us through, shouldn't it? Being kind, loving, caring, generous, happy pretty much covers the basics of life. Do we need a god or deity to determine life here and beyond?

It makes perfect sense to not need any type of god-like figure—as long as the ego is in control. Why should it matter? I am in charge, and I can control my destiny. Oh wait, destiny? Why is destiny in the equation? Whose destiny? Why is having a destiny or knowing about it even relevant? Something inside the spirit longs for a connection to something far beyond what this human journey offers. Mankind has searched for this answer throughout history. Each group that searches finds something to latch onto. When we believe we have found our inner mantra of what life is all about, we create a belief system or theology to support it—and then we follow the rules to keep us there.

Maybe in the brilliance of the plan of this human experiment, the whole idea is to find the way home. If in the description of what was considered the moment of separation of man from God, what would make the connection whole again? If religion teaches that we are sinners and going to some sort of hell after we die, what defines or measures us to not have to go to this hell? Follow the rules? Whose rules? And which one is even right about the rules? Does each group get to make its own rules? What are the rules about connecting to God anyway?

In the Old Testament, it doesn't take long to figure out that whoever controlled the land and defined the path to God would get to set the rules. Those who apparently had been chosen by God to establish law and order defined what was acceptable and what was not before this almighty deity. Step out of line—and lights out. Stay in line—and you get a reward. Really? A reward for what? If the king or guy in charge didn't like you, you were done.

How come the ones in charge got to determine the rules? Add a layer of religious influence, and suddenly you have a recipe that keeps everyone in line according to someone's standards or expectations.

If you create a structure that defines your eternal existence in the hereafter, you will maintain control of your own ego's mantra: me, myself, and I. This silly example plays itself out over and over again in the biblical narrative. Man believes God has given him the code. Man lives in fear of the God who decreed the code. Man will interpret the code to mean that he must stay in good standing with this God or else. All throughout the Old Testament, we see this battle of who is right and who is wrong. Those who believed they were in the right before God felt privileged to destroy anything that appeared to be evil or wrong. It was quite the system. Judgment is the operational word for determining the outcome of all those who are out of line.

A common theme runs through the Old Testament. No matter what the circumstances were or who was in charge, the same game played out over and over again. The human ego needed self-preservation. The best way to continue the mantra of the ego was to create fear in as many people as possible. Converting the fear into guilt created a form of control. Control manipulated with grimacing smiles, pretending to make the ego believe that it was doing the right thing for itself. If there was nothing to challenge that belief, the end result was manipulation at its finest.

If I am able to use fear as a weapon to bring guilt upon you, I will be able to control your life. If you allow me to use fear as a weapon, you will live with guilt—and your life will be controlled. This is not the same as self-control; it is nothing more than a form of witchcraft.

Doesn't guilt remind people that they have done something that is out of line, wrong, or illegal? Something within us triggers the spirit and causes us to rethink our actions or behaviors. This internal check comes from somewhere. A grid of life inside us counters the ego's dark side. The ego also knows that there is more. Sadly, the ego will usually take the approach that it is innocent. It will only come clean when it is confronted by the internal check of the conscience. Even when it is caught, it will try to wriggle its way out of being accountable. The idea of having to face the truth is ugly for the ego. It knows it will lose face and not be as in control as it believes it is.

Jim Carrey played a lawyer in *Liar Liar.* He was faced with having to tell the truth about everything. He is confronted with his own ego-driven lust for position and power. When he came to the realization that he could not escape the inner turmoil, he embraced the realm of what the spirit side of life was all about. His awakening was defined by one simple statement that his character makes. "And the truth shall set you free." What was the truth he was referring to? What is it about this statement that when we are confronted with the message and it hits home, we feel completely different? Life feels lighter, smiles become bigger, and things feel okay. Angst within us dissipates. Something begins to percolate, and the world looks and becomes different.

I was having a coffee with a friend, and we were discussing what is acceptable and what is not. Joe works with at-risk youth. These kids have experienced pretty much everything life can throw at them. Drugs, gangs, the harshness of the street, and fill in anything else you can come up with. He and a young man were discussing legalizing drugs. The young man thought that legalizing drugs was perfectly fine and not damaging to society, himself, or anyone else. It would be a way to solve the war on drugs by making it legal.

Joe took the position that it wasn't in the best interest to allow drugs to be normalized in society. He knew its effects and damage to people. The persistence of the other fellow in rationalizing his wanting to use drugs and have them become legal was mostly to justify his position.

Joe decided to throw a curveball and paint a picture of where the line might be if the wish was granted to legalize drugs and change our values around the use of drugs. The young man was so convinced that the way was to decriminalize drugs until he was confronted with the possibility that it might be more than what he was prepared for. Joe, bless his soul, played the devil's advocate and painted a picture for this young man. He put himself into character and played the part of the young man's little sister whom could now use these drugs when they became legal.

Joe said the look in the young man's eyes was piercing. His demeanor changed, and anger welled up at the idea of his little sister doing drugs. He was ready to attack Joe at the very thought of his little sister taking drugs—even if they were legal. The disconnect in the soul of the young man was so strong that his primary response mechanism was to attack and self-preserve. Where did his anger come from? All Joe did was paint a picture of a possible scenario that could play out. The young man's logic didn't want to allow for those he cared for to experience something possibly damaging that these drugs were capable of.

The ego believes it can create rules that only apply to a certain set of parameters. It has to. It cannot see beyond the selfish motivation it brings to the table. Joe was trying to show the young man that what you ask for could have far-reaching consequences—and you might not like the consequences once you get your wish. You might think you are asking for the right thing, but the hidden agenda usually reveals a much bigger challenge. The challenge often shows up as unintended consequences.

This can happen when we create rules and attempt to govern with the logic of the ego. All Joe did was try to get the young man to see beyond his frame of reference. Joe was taken aback by the young man's reaction to the possible consequences. Through the eyes of the ego, we justify and rationalize what we believe is the line. This line is defined by a limited separate state where the ego lives and exists.

Why did this young man react in such a fashion? What fueled his instant anger over the idea that his little sister could take this potentially legal drug and use it as she wished? The truth is that it had nothing to do with legalizing his drug of choice—or what may or may not be legal. He was formulating his decisions based upon an ego, which was in a state of separation and self-preservation, and using it as his guiding inner voice.

No matter the situation, when the same logic is applied by the ego, we will attack in an instant if it's going to make us look better. If we can argue our point of view, the ego will seize the moment. It will step across the line and snap with an answer or opinion that is driven to put the other down. It will, with little discernment, reveal judgment.

My friend Zahid facilitates a philosopher's café once a month. The topic of discussion is varied, and the rules are simple. No debate. You can bring your point of view and give your opinion, but debate is not encouraged. The reason is simple. Debate will go off in rabbit trails, and the focus of the discussion will lose it purpose. The biggest benefit of leaving debate at the door is to do one thing: listen.

Listening to varied perspectives and opinions forces us to confront our limited grasp or position on any given topic. Our values and beliefs will be confronted by what someone else may believe. For an hour and a half, debate is shelved. Listening with no judgments is difficult for the ego to embrace. The conscious practice of no judgments is one the ego would rather not confront.

During one of these discussions, I refrained from making any comments or opinion. I just sat and listened the whole time. I wanted to make some comments, but something inside told me to just listen this time. It was interesting to hear how the discussion unfolded. The topic moved from opinion to commentary, and right smack in the middle, a debate ensued. In that moment, the dynamics shifted from open thought and comments to judgments about who was right or wrong. It was subtle at first, but it quickly became apparent that the original question posed to the group was of little value. It took a few moments, but the moderator caught it—and the group was brought back into focus.

None of us can escape what happened in this example. We do it constantly—or are at least constantly confronted by this dilemma. The moment we feel threatened by someone's point of view or perspective, we bite back with words and/or actions. Something inside us will be conflicted, whether we acknowledge it or not. The ego doesn't want to acknowledge that reality, and it will attempt to hide the motivation. We can run, but we can't hide. We find it difficult to resist the temptation to create judgments about something that stirs emotion within us. Positioning ourselves to make us feel "in the right" is what the ego is all about. It will reinforce the idea that we are separate from anything external and prolong the agony of isolation.

No matter the circumstances, we will always be confronted with the ego's first stance to be in the right. It happens at every level of our existence. This is one of the reasons I love what Zahid's philosophers café represents. The topic really doesn't matter. For sure, it is fun to give an opinion or ramble about something on which I may have a perspective, but the strength of the dialogue is in listening without judgment. I may even leave the meeting without agreeing with someone's point of view, but if I allow it, I may leave with an appreciation of the varied perspectives on life.

The biggest learning moment is being aware of how I respond internally to the discussion—and whether I can embrace the differences and allow myself to be stretched in my own mind—with my own belief systems and what I perceive to be my rules of life.

There is a common denominator we all carry in life. It matters not what kind of personality we have or how we see the world. We get to make decisions about what connects us to spirit that teaches us why we are here. This incredible design of the ego, soul, spirit, and mind determines our values and how we will live.

We attempt to compartmentalize life and create structures with black and white answers. This structure gives us certainty— or at least so we think it does. The funny thing is those whose personalities lend to structure and certainty usually are the ones who create the compartments because they are good at it.

On the other side of the coin are those who never want to be caught in a compartment. They refuse to be boxed in or feel like they are boxed in. The rainbow personality will want to chase wide-open spaces. They are good at pushing the edge of uncertainty. When the structured personality bumps against the rainbow personality, ideals and values lock horns. The crazy thing is that both need each other. When we recognize our unique gifts in life, we no longer judge. This is where "tension in harmony" makes its greatest impact. It assists us in our external world, and the dynamic has far greater effects upon the inner world where confrontations occur.

CHAPTER 11

Illusion and Timing

I would like to share with you a couple of stories that illustrate how life is lived. How are we motivated to do what we do? I want to give measure and perspective to what often happens in life when we consider the circumstances that shape who we are.

How often have you pursued something in life that you thought mattered, only to discover that what you were chasing was an illusion—something that never gave you what it promised? Oh, it looked good, but somehow in the end it just never measured up to the promise. What about circumstances in life that just seemed too odd and had a perplexity about them that seemed out of the ordinary? Do you recognize these experiences and let them teach you who you are and why you are here?

Why is illusion and timing relevant to what I'm attempting to communicate about guilt? Illusion is something the ego thrives on for its existence. Timing of life events confronts the ego in that there is something beyond itself that it cannot explain. It is in there that I would like to introduce and tease you about how meditation opens the door to removing the barrier that separation and isolation have existed under. You might be asking why I am weaving meditation into the topic and at this juncture. I want you to begin to see what happens as we consider how meditation shifts life. This is an introduction to the roadmap I'm preparing.

I have done commercial work in television and print media. This industry has learned how to create illusions. They show you only what the camera wants to show you. The medium is powerful. It captures our senses and emotions and makes them believe what we desire. I have a picture of me in a hot tub commercial with a lovely lady. We were in a hot tub with a lush palm tree backdrop. The photographer captured the perfect romantic moment. The odd thing is that the hot tub is barely shown in the picture. What was being marketed? Was it the tub? Was it an idea or a feeling? The image evoked strong feelings about what the product could do for you.

Men will have one idea, and the ladies will be thinking something completely different, but the end result is to get the potential purchaser to believe they will experience what the image is presenting. The truth of the photo is that we were in a hot tub in the middle of a warehouse. The room reeked of fiberglass, which was not the most pleasant of smells. The water was not the warmest, and after about ninety minutes in the tub, we felt like prunes. We kept smiling and giving the camera what it needed to make the moment work. I chuckle when I look at the picture. It reminds me of how we are drawn into the world of illusion and how the ego gets caught up in wanting not so much the product but what the product promises to achieve. The idea that the product, no matter what it is, will satisfy a deep-seated human need.

Marketing is brilliant at nudging the ego's belief that an illusion can be reality. It will even give the senses the satisfaction of the pleasure it promises, but the eyes long for something more elusive. The chase never ends. I wrote a song and called it "Chasing the World." The twist in the lyrics is that we see one thing, but something else is happening. The first two lines go like this:

Chasing the world ... chasing the dream.
No one knows if it's as real ... as real as it seems.

Illusion holds us in the belief that we will have everything and achieve everything while we are here on this planet. We will chase the dream because the ego believes the dream is all there is. This dream of illusion by the ego has no understanding of the spirit realm. It cannot. It was never designed to live in the realm of spirit; therefore, it will subjugate every decision to the rules it lives under. In the world of illusion, we search and search, but we never find. The idea of illusion keeps us suspicious. Illusionists are very skilled at creating distractions. They will create a preoccupation with something that distracts the viewer and use diversions to accomplish their goals. Their sole purpose is to convince you that what they did was magical. The deception is brilliant.

Magicians use illusions to create distractions. We are intrigued by what the illusions offer. We find the attraction in the unknown. We like to be in control, but somehow we are attracted to the feeling of being out of control when it comes to illusions. They have the ability to capture our attention and make us believe one thing while accomplishing something else.

What is the purpose of an illusion by a skilled magician? Is it designed to entertain us? Is it designed to reveal something about us? Does the sleight of hand or tricking the eyes tell us more about ourselves or the one doing the trick?

The ego has a way of creating a busy life by formulating problems that it wants us to answer. The preoccupation with diversionary tactics throws us off and keeps the mind confused. The ego's tactics are simple. It will convince us that this body we live in is all there is. It will shower us with promises of protection, assurance, and answers to life. The ego has no other option because it cannot believe that eternity or the possibility of life beyond here exists.

The ego will create a structure to offer the possibility of eternity. It goes to great lengths to formulate constructs that try desperately to answer life's questions. Since the ego cannot connect with spirit, it must find ways to keep the mind occupied with what it believes is tangible. We can find examples of how the ego demonstrates the motives of life. As long as it confuses the mind enough to keep it guessing, it will remain in control.

It will stay in that place where the mind is continually fed a smorgasbord of contradiction.

In the contradiction, the ego laughs at the soul and keeps us in isolation. Its ultimate goal is separation. The ego is skilled at keeping us out of balance. It has no intention of allowing us to have awareness about anything. If we become aware of life and our true journey here, the ego will sabotage us—without any regard for the consequences. I mentioned earlier how the need to judge is right at the doorstep of the mind. The ego will believe it judges rightly, but when confronted by the soul/spirit, it cowers and runs for cover. If the ego allowed sane judgment the opportunity to manifest itself, it would be terminated in its ability to control to the degree it wants to, which is not a pretty sight for the ego. The ego—and what it believes about how life should be lived—is a life of contradiction.

The ego doesn't consider life beyond this life. If it did, it would have to admit that it has little value in its existence. However, the ego knows that life is much more than the illusion it offers. Knowing it cannot escape the reality of its mortal condition, it will concoct theories, theologies, concepts, and ideas to show that in spite of the ego's limitations, it can prove that our defined existence will have rules that are governed by what the ego determines acceptable.

The full-circle approach the ego takes is simple: Take control, manipulate, confuse, dissociate, unsettle, contradict, distort, and with a dash of a smile, sneer at the very idea that there is life beyond the body. Finally, bake it all together until the judgmental flavors are permeating throughout every pore of the soul. This is the recipe on which the ego thrives and keeps us living in isolation and separation. It's a nice meal if death is your ultimate purpose.

Have you ever been caught by surprise or had something happen at just the right moment? We walk across the street at just a certain time, make a phone call, or turn left instead of right. We don't always recognize our actions in the moments they occur. We sometimes realize them after the fact: a chance meeting, a change in direction, or a whole new path.

Sometimes what appear to be backward steps may be moving us forward—faster than we could have ever imagined. The timing of events—when recognized as something orchestrated by something beyond our rational, logical mind—is flavored with mystery. What is this mystery? Why does it reveal itself the way it does? What do these experiences teach us about the journey? Do they matter? Do we recognize them when they appear? Do we recognize that something beyond human comprehension is assisting us in the journey?

I've always believed that life is not random—and that life has a way of bringing us the things we need at just the right moments. The timing of events is enhanced when we have a spiritual understanding and connection to what the spirit life is all about. This mystery of life is something to behold when we experience those moments and wonder how things happened. How did the circumstances navigate themselves to accomplish that task? The cool thing is that we get to be the focus of this mystery and participate in the magic of the moment.

I do not ask for miracles anymore. Aren't we supposed to ask for miracles? We all want them. If not for ourselves, we want them for someone else, especially for those who may need a miracle.

I don't ask for miracles anymore. I just ask "Which part and what role of the miracle am I?". Do you see the difference? Miracles are all around us—all the time, constantly. Do we see them? Do we recognize them when they occur? Have we positioned ourselves to be in that place when they show up?

What are miracles? How do we define them? A **miracle** is defined by an event not explicable by natural or scientific laws. We attribute these kinds of events to a supernatural being (God or gods), a miracle worker, a saint or even a religious leader. The word "miracle" is often used to characterize any beneficial event that is considered unlikely but not in contradiction to the laws of nature, such as surviving a natural disaster, or simply a "wonderful" occurrence. Other miracles might be: survival of an illness diagnosed as terminal, escaping a life-threatening situation or 'beating the odds'. Sometimes coincidences are seen as miracles.

Miracles are not difficult for the realm of spirit to orchestrate. What is much more astounding is how we position ourselves in life to have a role in someone else's miracle. It can be overwhelming to the soul when we know that we were a part of someone's miracle. The spirit gets lifted to new heights of awareness. In this awareness, the ego becomes unglued because the realm of spirit changes life, sets new courses, and turns our eyes to look beyond the limitations of the journey often determined by the ego.

These experiences teach us that time here is measured with precision. Miracles may not always show up when we think they should. Events have layers of mystery that are orchestrated with a comprehension of what is in the past, present, and future. They are wrapped together, drawn into a moment of time where we get to intersect with and in. The more we find ourselves in a place of connection with spirit, the more the wonders of life occur.

Miracles can appear insignificant and be brushed off, but at other times, they can be catalysts for someone's significant miracle, which can change everything for them. When we are available to be part of a miracle, the world changes. The ego is unable to rationalize the experience and will attempt to minimize the impact and the moment. In those moments, the ego will rationalize the experiences as freaky circumstances randomly happened without anything else influencing the events. It is in this realm where life is confronted about whom gets to lead. The ego or the spirit.

Several years ago I purchased an acreage. The yard was a mess and needed a lot of help to bring it back to the beauty it once held. In early November, I was moving some plants around to make the yard a bit more attractive. I had an old greenhouse in the middle of my yard. It wasn't the prettiest greenhouse, and it really needed some TLC. As I was moving the plants around, I turned around to face the greenhouse. Something inside triggered me to make an odd request. I knew instantly that there was a prompting, but the prompting seemed goofy. I thought I was thinking something that was odd, quirky, and childish. I was frozen for a moment. I gazed at the greenhouse and exclaimed, "I would like two cedar hedges for the greenhouse—one on each corner—and I would like them for Christmas."

I laughed inside as I finished my declaration. I was thinking that two cedar hedges would soften the harsh look of the building. I had an inner dialogue. My ego began to mock my mind. The request sounded insane, according to the ego's logic and reason.

I started to doubt the declaration and looked for the logic in the request. Why did I make the request? Why would something so insignificant matter in this world where there are world wars, famines, and other things that are way more important to the realm of spirit and relevance to our existence here?

Did something in my spirit touch something beyond me in that moment? If it did, it sure gave me the impression my request mattered. The following weeks had my mind racing. I thought my mind was playing tricks on me. We often get nudges within us when the ego attempts to discard the moment with its own rationalization of the possibility of losing its position within our existence. The ego cannot come to terms with these moments that interfere with its agenda.

A few weeks later, I saw a sign for cedar hedges. I dialed the number and asked the guy if he would sell me a couple of hedges. They were pretty cheap around there. I took matters into my own hands and followed through on my request by doing it the way we do things on this planet. Makes sense, doesn't it? It falls perfectly into how the ego frames everything we do. We take charge and stay in control of what happens. Silly me! I should have known better. I knew in my spirit that it was outside my human logic, but something a few weeks back had nudged me to see this differently.

The guy said it was too wet, but I should call him in the spring when it was drier. When he hung up the phone, I wondered why he wouldn't sell me the hedges. Crazy. That was his chance to make a few bucks—and he hung up on me.

I decided to let things unfold. I was trying to grasp the idea of two cedar hedges showing up for Christmas without interfering in the process, which was not easy to do when logic and reasoning are challenged and the ego is unable to accept what appears illogical.

The closer Christmas got, the more I thought I had missed something. Maybe something in my spirit was off. Maybe I was partly delusional. Maybe I misunderstood the message—and I had wished for something that was nonsensical.

When was the last time you experienced that kind of moment and brushed it off? Did you think you were losing your mind and probably wouldn't be a good idea to tell your friends? On the day before Christmas, I saw no cedar hedges.

In my mind, a voice said, "See, Alvin? You were wrong. You didn't really hear anything, and there are no hedges coming. Just forget about it. Carry on. You don't need that spirit stuff to mess you up. You have only you—and that's all you need." The ego loves to play with our insecurities.

Christmas morning was beautiful. The kids started the day by opening their gifts, and we enjoyed the moment. By ten, the gifts were all torn open and the kids were having fun playing. I needed a cup of coffee. I sat down at the kitchen table with my coffee and was enjoying watching the kids play. I looked out my kitchen window and looked across my yard. My greenhouse was as tacky as ever, and I realized that no cedar hedges would be there until spring. I looked up over the trees that bordered my neighbor's yard and saw smoke rising above the tree line. My first thought that hit me was that the smoke must be coming from my neighbor's burning barrel. I thought he was probably burning his Christmas wrappings. The next thought burned into me even more—no pun intended—was that I should go say Merry Christmas to my neighbor.

I put on my shoes and walked to my neighbor's yard. Sure enough, Gord was burning his Christmas wrappings. I wished him a Merry Christmas, and we began to chitchat about life. About a minute into our conversation, Gord said something that would change my world forever. I learned that the realm of spirit is far more connected to us than I often realize and how timing of life events will reveal themselves when spirit directs.

The night before, after the Christmas Eve church service, Gord helped clean up the stage and put away the props. Another helper said to Gord who is a hobby gardener and a plant collector, told him to take the plants home that were part of the production. His next words sent my mind spinning. Gord pointed at a pair of potted cedar hedges by his garage and said, "See those two cedar hedges? Would you like to take those cedar hedges home?"

In that brief moment, my mind went into overdrive. My jaw dropped and I said yes. I was in a foggy state, messages ran through my mind, and tingly sensations covered my skin. I knew something was unfolding that had layers of mystery.

I said I would get my wheelbarrow to bring the hedges home.

He said, "Do it tomorrow. Sounds like work for a Christmas day when you should be relaxing."

I was vibrating inside and said, "You don't understand. I need to do this now."

I raced home and grabbed my wheelbarrow. I wasn't exactly focused on pushing a wheelbarrow down the street on Christmas morning. I'm sure my neighbors were wondering what on earth I was doing, especially when I came back with two cedar hedges bouncing in my wheelbarrow. I grabbed my shovel, dug two holes, and gently placed the two unique cedar hedges into their new permanent home.

Nothing was going to stop that moment from happening. It was just two silly cedars that stood four feet high and mattered very little to the world of plants. They grow like weeds on the West Coast. That morning, everything was different. I finished my task, put away my shovel and wheelbarrow, and walked back to my house. I turned around and looked at the two cedars. I looked at my watch, and my heart skipped a beat. My watch said 11:00 AM Christmas morning.

I fell on my knees and allowed my mind to race as fast as it could as I tried to comprehend the logistics of what had occurred. Not only was the original message that I was to have two cedar hedges for Christmas, but they showed up on Christmas morning with such precision that I could never come up with such a complex set of circumstances. The spirit realm wanted to teach me about perfect timing, who we are, and being connected to something beyond the ego's concept of life on earth. I always knew timing mattered, but I didn't fully comprehend how precise and definitive the timing can be when our spirit engages with the realm of spirit that longs to assist us through the journey.

Remember those credit card ads we used to see on TV? Cedar hedges: 20 bucks. Shovel: 15 dollars. Two cedar hedges showing up Christmas morning: priceless.

A while later, I began to contemplate the circumstances and logistics that came together to fulfill the moment for me. My miracle. How many people actually played a role without ever knowing what was happening in my world? Those who designed the evening service. Someone who had the hedges and offered them to the event. Gord offering to help clean up. Someone suggesting that Gord take home the plants. And I happened to be sitting at my kitchen table at just the moment Gord was burning his paper wrappings. The nudge within me to go and say Merry Christmas to my neighbor. These little moments in the journey from me asking for two silly hedges in early November to receiving this perfectly timed gift at just the right moment—not a day before, not a day after. I received the most amazing gift of all that perfect morning, just after all the gifts had been opened.

I tell you this story because there are usually many dynamics occurring in life on several levels and layers—all at the same time. How often do we ignore that voice inside because we think it is silly or nonsensical? The ego dislikes that part of the world because it has to acknowledge a dynamic that includes a spiritual connection. Life is measured and defined in that spiritual connection.

CHAPTER 12

Why You Matter

I want you to discover the journey of the spiritual connection. It is not just in experience; but in how we live life every day. When we discover this side of life and let ourselves be shaped by what is going on in the spirit, everything changes. Once we embrace that part of life, we know we can never go back to letting the ego dictate our reactions or responses. Everything changes and looks different through a new lens.

The journey through the spirit doesn't take away the complexities of life. The challenges still show up, and some will even become more pronounced. The ego will make sure of that because it knows it is losing control. It wants to protect itself and tell the mind that it will protect the body. If it has to, it will create as much conflict as it can to prove its value. The perceived and believed value that the ego relies upon will attempt to make illusion the reality it thinks exists. As we reorient our internal thinking structure, a shift occurs within—and something new begins. We define and experience mysteries in new ways, and miracles reveal themselves.

I was privileged to have several people play roles in my cedar hedge miracle. Most of those involved wouldn't have even realized it. It's amazing how this happens—and how much more often when we put ourselves in that place when we get to play a role in everyday miracles. We will be aware of some of the miracles, but we won't see or know about many others. The central focus of life is intentionally structuring the world to allow the spirit to connect and experience life in ways that boggle the mind.

In the life of spirit, guilt has no hold. It cannot. There is no guilt in the realm of connection to what is defined by living in the realm of a spiritual connection, but it raises many questions. *What spirit? To whose spirit am I connecting? Can I know for sure what this looks like? Will it make me look like a weirdo? Can I trust this connection? How do we connect? Is it another religious exercise?*

Many people have the idea that our personalities are defined by a combination of emotional, attitudinal, and behavioral response patterns. The thought is that children have a temperament, and that personalities don't fully mature until later in life. I'm not convinced. I think personalities are defined the day we show up on this planet. I think our personalities are our signatures in life and are unique. However, the personality often gets downplayed or not considered as relevant as it ought to be. We are quick to compare each other—often against each other—and attempt to make others be like someone else. We try to make ourselves be like someone else—even behaving like them. Comparing usually leads to judgment and prejudice.

I think our personalities are to be honored and respected. Respect who we are and what we bring to this world. We are unique, and our personalities are gifts to those we encounter. Those unique personality traits give us tools to find out how to connect with this journey and how to meet the challenges we face.

There is a lot of material already written about personalities and personality testing. I won't go into detail about the dynamics of how we identify our strengths and weaknesses, but I want to give some context and explain why I believe that personality is more relevant to our growth than we realize.

The complexity of who we are is astounding. We have several layers that are wrapped up into a physical frame. The mind, ego, spirit, and soul could be other pieces. Beyond those layers of what makes the human entity exist, is the personality. Look around and observe how we interact with one another. Observe how we consider events, situations, beliefs, and behaviors. They often determine our positions in relation to our personalities.

Notice how we are attracted to some personalities, and we shy away from others. We find ourselves attracted to certain people, and their personalities play a significant role in that attraction. The ones we find ourselves in conflict with usually teach us the most about ourselves. This unique design of our existence creates a mosaic of dynamics that beg us to consider how the signature of our personality moves us through this journey.

One of the challenges we face is how we measure each other. Some people are given skills and talents to make technical decisions and think in a very sequential manner. The world is structured, and they usually have strong convictions about how order is manifested. Others have skills and talents that are defined by what I call the colors of the rainbow. They are the artists, and the colors they see blur together. It gives their personalities the flavors they need to fulfill their roles on this planet. Inside this range, a variety of personality mixes have been designed to give a full expression to our experiences here.

The challenge we all have is to honor one another in the uniqueness of what we bring as our gifts. In this point of view, I introduce the role of meditation, what it represents, and why it matters. We can all experience the same level of spiritual life, reflecting the same level of respect toward one another. Judgments diminish because we are all on the same level in the spiritual life.

CHAPTER 13

Meditation and Life

Meditation is a practice that has been around for a long time. Those who practice meditation express it in many variations. I would like to connect you to an expression of the practice of meditation.

Where does meditation fit into the world of guilt? How does it affect the moral code or human disposition? Guilt shapes us and is used by the ego because it believes it is separate from any other influence. Meditation is the vehicle that takes us from what is ego-driven self-preservation to spirit connection and possibility. The spirit was designed to live in connection, and this longing within us searches for its home.

The spirit can be squashed or beaten down, but it will never be decimated because the conscience we carry within us knows there is more to life than what we are told by the ego. The complexity and brilliance of being a human creation is astounding. Think about all the layers that define how we make decisions, what motivates us to do what we do, and the capacity to reason and think. Our physical abilities and limitations have creative capacity when choices are placed in front of us. That capacity is amazing. Now, add the mechanisms within us to take the whole array of this layering of capacity and see how our minds, spirits, souls, egos, senses, and brains attempt to correlate all the information to make sense of what we are doing here and where this journey is taking us. It is incredible that we manage as well as we do.

The dynamic between the ego and spirit is the primary focal point. In that room, the ego creates a boxing ring and attempts to keep the spirit out of balance. We have heard the term that some people have gentle spirits and others are mean spirited. Where does that come from? Don't we all have the same spirit DNA within us? Have you ever found yourself being mean spirited and flipping into a gentle spirit almost seamlessly? Or vice versa.

We can be kind and loving, and something flips us upside-down, and we lash out with rage and despair. This trigger comes from somewhere. If this trigger has no governing mechanism to assess, the consequences may be more than we can bear. Why does the conscience poke back at the reactive stance? What fuels the conscience to quicken the mind and consider a different outcome? Are we designed to live with no external help from beyond the human system?

If we come to the conclusion that it is purely up to us in human form to determine any outcome that we want, we have the recipe for a belief system that relies on what is determined provable. No potential god or external influence other than what we know here as logic and reason shaped by our knowledge and opinion will determine what we think is true. The last breath is the last breath, and nothing else matters but what we experience on this planet. The ego thrives in this condition because it believes it has no guilt—all the while judging with the harshest of consequences toward anyone who doesn't believe what the one judging has determined the rules to be. Performance within the rules is the measuring stick. Dance the dance, and you will get a reward.

When the conscience calls for some other response, it is appealing to the spirit for help. The conflict can be overwhelming, but the spirit is not dictatorial because its very design is to live in a place of connection beyond the self. This internal jostling of ego versus the spirit is the core of humanity's' existence.

The ego demands, and the spirit invites. When the spirit invites, what is it inviting? I would suggest that the invitation is to connect with spirit. There has been much discussion over the years about spirit guides, what they do, and how they operate. I invite you to journey with me to discover a spirit guide like no other. This spirit guide isn't restricted by the past, present, or future. It has no limitations to understanding, knowledge, or wisdom. Does it sound too good to be true? It is true. Alvin, how do you know, prove it? You want proof; humor me through these pages while I take you on a journey.

Meditation is the vehicle that opens up the world of spirit and reveals the mystery of life. The ego wants definitive answers and logic, and the spirit longs for a connection with the miraculous. The spirit thrives in this realm. It is in the connection of the spirit with the Holy Spirit that makes it all work. What or whom is the Holy Spirit—and what does that mean anyway? It sounds religious doesn't it. The Holy Spirit embraced as a guide for life means that we must consider our belief systems. What do we believe about life beyond the human experience? We are free to believe as we choose. The ego will make sure it has a say, but the spirit will invite us to consider the relationship where it longs to be connected. Our spirit recognizes this link and will search out its whole life—if needed—to discover it.

Who is this Holy Spirit? Religions define the Holy Spirit as the divine aspect of prophecy and wisdom. the divine force, quality, and influence from God. What does the Holy Spirit teach? His teaching is to undo a life of guilt and bring healing. The Holy Spirit knows only but the spirit as you. His gift is for you to accept His vision as yours. Always remember, the Holy Spirit's love is your strength.

Our response to everything in life connects directly to our interpretations of life events. Here is where we find justification for our responses. When we feel attacked, deserted, or controlled, we behave as if it is truly so. The ego attempts to make it real and gives power to what is perceived. Ego motivation has layers of complexity that are difficult to track. The only place we get to make a decision about our motivation is within the mind. The mind determines what we believe. We will either believe in the script of the ego—or we will consider the invitation that comes by way of the spirit.

When we allow the Holy Spirit to walk alongside us, we filter life through a very different lens. We will be given wisdom and understanding of what is ours because it is in the essence of the Holy Spirit to live from the eternal value and nature of what is Truth. The more we lean into the influence of the Holy Spirit, the more we find ourselves relinquishing the judgments through ego-driven perceptions. The amazing part is that the Holy Spirit's judgment requires no effort or strain. With the absence of love as our motivation, fear will motivate and we will remain locked into a constant cry for help.

Why do we cry for help? We desire healing, wholeness, and connection. There are only two emotions we are capable of feeling: fear and love. Fear lives in denial. Love holds truth. This is the simplest of plans ever laid out for us in this journey. We fear what we do not know. The ego knows not of love; it places conditions on love to make it think it has it sorted out. Religion, when messed up by the ego's agenda, twists the truth, and love's conflicting messages confuse the mind into believing the message of the ego.

As we recognize fear and remove the disguises, we embrace the undoing of the ego. This undoing gives the spirit the ability to grow. All that is required from us is to accept the gift that the Holy Spirit offers. His gift is to remove the separation in which the ego thrives. If we perceive a world of separation, we will live under constant attack.

The mind is our decision-making mechanism over which we have no control. We determine what is truth and what we deny. We can deny pretty much anything we want, but we cannot deny that there is more than just what the ego can offer. We can choose the world we make up—or we can choose the world that truly exists.

The world of ego is driven to lead us to futility and depression. Why is the field of mental health growing so rapidly? The diagnoses of clinical depression, anxiety, and conflict are gaining momentum. If we approach the diagnosis of ego-masked mental illnesses, we will rarely touch the surface of what is at the heart of the matter.

Life in the realm of spirit is not for the faint of heart. It is all about your heart. Religion offers a mask to satisfy the ego's attempt to go along with the game. The Holy Spirit's plan is simple. In our will is spirit, and in the will is the "price" of what awaits us. It seems silly to invest in what the ego plans to give us. Why wouldn't we want what gives life? Yet, the power of fear and control over us is often more tempting than embracing something that brings us peace, joy, and contentment.

It is stated by the World Health Organization that mental health will be the second biggest cause of death by 2020. (http://www.irishhealth.com/article.html?id=1447)

If mental health is now affecting more than 400 million people and growing, what happens when we get to the tipping point? Will we all be insane? What drives mental health and this increasing awareness that something is going drastically wrong?

Very few people want to be religious, and for many, the idea that God is not a harsh judging figurehead or a gray-bearded old man is difficult to behold and embrace. Too much of what our world has encountered is a twisted form of what is offered through the spirit, and the ego has masterfully conflicted our relationships with spirit.

The ego has convinced us that we can have it all. The world is our oyster, and our success will be defined by the accomplishments we achieve. As long as something is perceived as more valuable than your soul, you will remain convinced that your soul can be bought or sold. The Holy Spirit has one goal. That is to awaken your soul to its real potential. This awakening or accepting of the vision of the Holy Spirit changes everything. We are given the real world through the Holy Spirit in exchange for this world we made up. The whole gig is designed for us to find the way back home—and back to what was never lost. When we choose to remember who we really are, we give up controlling this insane idea about what the world offers through the lens of the ego.

The ego is unable to betray God, but it will betray us because it defines itself by the measurement of being treacherous. The Holy Spirit's work is solely focused on undoing this guilt. This is the tiptoeing the ego takes as it attempts to keep us guilty. It will remind us at every chance that we have been treacherous, especially to God. This treacherous behavior is deserving of death, and the ego will happily oblige.

The twist in the ego's logic is that it will convince you that this guilt came from God. Where else would it even consider this? It has no other option because its whole agenda is for self-preservation, and it will cast blame on someone or something else. Knowing this, it will play right into the mad idea that the best thing to do would be to kill the soul—or at least confuse it enough to mess up the mind and make it appear as if it's gone insane. It sounds a lot like what is happening all around us in through the challenges of what is happening in the field of mental health. According to the World Health Organization, it is becoming an epidemic.

Okay. I have deviated from where I was a ways back. I was introducing the idea of how meditation fits into this whole scheme. I wanted to un-package and give context of where I am coming from and where I am heading with this idea of how guilt plays so well into our motivation of life and how we determine how our morality will define our mortality and how our mortality defines our morality.

The art of meditation is varied in form, but the consistent nature of meditation takes us to the place where we connect with spirit. When we think of meditation, we often have an image of a serene, pastoral scene far away from the hustle and bustle of life. Google the word *meditation,* and most of the images show a person wearing light clothing, sitting in some sort of meditative legs-crossed position, and usually staring off into a sunset, lake, or mountain meadow. Meditation has been around for thousands of years. The modern era of Western meditation practices tends to focus on self-awareness for stress reduction and relaxation. A calming of the mind helps people deal with life's challenges. Our modern era of meditation focuses more on self-awareness than on the spiritual dynamic. I wonder if it is because the nature of spirituality in the modern world has been influenced too much by religion.

Spirituality hasn't exactly been the criteria for measuring success or been looked upon as something to be desired. Those who are seen as spiritual seekers often come across as being too emotional for the world. Not managing our affairs on our own is a sign of weakness or a crutch. I wonder if the avoidance of being spiritual in meditation is too wide open for the one meditating.

If one meditates, what or who is one directing the meditation toward? Are we just considering our internal world, creating our wishes of life, and zeroing in on the list we compile? Who or what motivates our internal list of what we want? What do we open ourselves up to? What do we want to open ourselves up to?

In the realm of spirit, there will be influences that serve us well, but there may also be false spirits that will influence. How do we know the difference? Is there a difference? The minute one embraces the spirit realm, the spirit guides reveal themselves. There is much written and spoken about when it comes to spirit guides. My intent here is to not debate the dynamics of what this area of spirit encompasses. My focus will remain where I believe the world of spirit calls with certainty and can be trusted.

I have spent many years considering how the spirit fits into the journey. The spirit realm offers much. The challenge is to discern from where you connect the spirit to a spirit that will influence your life. The ego will play along with spirit—but only if it can determine which spirit will come along for the ride. The ego's deceptive nature will partner with a deceptive spirit and wreak havoc, which is worse than not having any spiritual connection.

This would be reason enough to stay away from any meditation and spirit connection because of the mess it can create. It's no wonder the modern era removes the idea of spirituality from meditation. If meditation stays under the control of the ego, discourse and confusion will still be in the equation. The practitioners will give up, and the experiences will leave them empty. We are extremely capable on our own. We can accomplish much without spiritual guidance. At least, we believe we can.

If we are only here to survive and live with little hope of anything beyond this journey, spiritual influence would be non-issue. Mental health practitioners would figure out the problems, and by all accounts, they should be our leaders. The drug companies would be our best investment because they will have the pill solution to our anxiety about life. I realize I am being somewhat facetious here. I hope you get my drift.

I invite you to consider the Holy Spirit as your guide to assist you in this journey. His understanding of the past, present, and future has all the wealth of wisdom and understanding that will assist us as we make choices about life and how we respond to each other in this journey. His goal is to assist us in finding our way home. The simple measuring tool for us is in how we allow love to be expressed and manifested in our lives. How fast are we able to let things go? Can we position ourselves to be conduits for miracles? Do we concern ourselves with judging others? We will still make judgments about the choices in front of us, but we will no longer judge each other by the ego's standards.

One of the fears in meditation is staying focused. We can be distracted in a moment. We think we are to empty the mind in meditation. I think not. I think meditation is about focusing on who and where the journey is taking us. Learning to focus in the practice is a learned behavior. It is a mechanical principal. As one learns to meditate, the focus becomes clearer. Even when we are on our game in meditation, we can still be distracted in a moment. The trick is to not panic or feel defeated. The simple process is to go back to where you were and/or find the awakened moment because the distraction may have actually given you more on which to meditate on. It is learning to be aware—not just self-aware—but aware of the connection between the Holy Spirit and your own spirit.

The mind will begin to see the unlimited possibilities of what is available in life. Is structure important? Is structure restrictive or supportive? Sometimes both. Structure creates a place for the mechanics of meditation to operate. If structure impedes the moment and creative elements in meditation, it should be set aside.

I like to practice meditation in formal and informal spaces of time. I take blocks of time to focus on my practice or ritual in structure in order to take in the full expression of the value I place on this form of meditation. I keep the meditative practice awake at all times. Whether I am busy working, sitting in a meeting, or having fun and relaxing, I try to be ready to be a part of any possible miracle. It is a fun way to live. Anywhere you go, you get to be a conduit for someone's miracle—and you know it when it happens.

How many miracles have we missed when we downplayed or minimized the influence that the Holy Spirit can have in our lives? For a moment, set aside the idea of what miracles look like or represent. Consider what happens through your life when you allow the Holy Spirit to orchestrate events, coordinate dreams, all the while , giving us peace in our soul, knowing that life will work out.

This journey isn't about being cozy or cute and having a white picket fence. The journey will be filled with complexity and challenges, many of which will bring us to the point of exhaustion and hopelessness. This is all the more reason to have the Holy Spirit guide the journey and give us the resources and tools to live our lives to the max. Is our goal on this planet to acquire the right portfolio and end up with a retirement package that drifts us off into the sunset?

At the time of this writing, it was just announced that Nelson Mandela passed away. He breathed his last. The biggest compliment I read about Nelson was his impact to help change the world, to be respectful toward each other, and to treat each other with respect. He was a world hero by most standards, but the world he lived in treated him as a criminal. He spent the better part of twenty-seven of his ninety-five years imprisoned for believing in and wanting to achieve a measure of peace and safety for millions of people. Go figure. Why would the world he tried to change for the better treat him with such disdain?

The world does not promise happiness and easy, self-made millions that marketing campaigns promise. We are here to learn and discover how to dismantle the barriers that guilt places upon us and be conduits for miracles upon miracles. Nelson Mandela was as human as the rest of us, but in, he understood that miracles would occur if he allowed truth to shape his spirit. Death will consume those who choose to live by the dictate of the ego. Those whose light shines bright will scatter what is darkened by the illusion the ego creates.

CHAPTER 14

Meditation and Mechanics

There are mechanics that make meditation work well. I see meditation just as I see West Coast swing dancing. I found the analogy so similar to meditation that I couldn't resist bringing the two together. Recently, Jacquie and I went into dance lessons with very little knowledge of how to dance to West Coast swing style.

I was pretty much off the scale when it came to understanding how to dance this style. Jacquie, on the other hand, was quite proficient at the art. Her coordination and style had most students looking like complete rookies. I was the rookie of all rookies. In the first lesson, the instructor had us learn to count. One … two … three and four … five and six. It was not a problem, but it did require focus—and it took a while to feel the rhythm.

In the next lesson, she added some steps with this counting. I hoped my two left feet and my head would be able to pull it off. Counting and moving the feet and body in sequence can be difficult when one has to think, focus, and actually make it happen. It can be a bit overwhelming, and it does look quite funny.

I attempted to do a step where we had to count and move a certain way. My brain was thinking the opposite to what my feet and body were trying to accomplish. The instructor looked over at me and attempted to correct my movements in a very kind way. The problem was that my brain had no capability to actually align itself with what the instructor was saying—or what my feet were doing.

She tried to gracefully adjust my movements. By the third try, I was too far away from the message. I watched my feet go in contradictory directions. She started laughing because it really did look funny. She and many other dancers had grins. Some were trying to be polite, but my goofiness was a bit over the top. Even I couldn't resist laughing at my brain's inability to synchronize with my feet. After much laughter, I managed to finally get it working right. So much for simple dance lessons.

The third thing she taught us was adding a partner. I was somewhat nervous, although I knew full well that the moment would come. I took Jacquie's hand. The music started, and off we went with our awkward counting, stepping, and movements. I must have looked like a high school kid at his first dance. It was fun, but it did take a while to get the hang of combining the steps and movements with a partner. It was going okay, but I noticed something as we switched from dance partner to dance partner. It was easy to dance with some, but with others, it felt awkward. I didn't know what made the difference. I just thought that maybe some could dance and others couldn't—or maybe it was me. Maybe I wasn't quite getting it.

The instructor told us there was one more step. She said it would make all the difference. Now she had my attention. I wanted to know. I wanted to know how to dance properly and be good at it. It was pretty much mechanical up until then; she got my attention when she said the next lesson would make it all work.

She said the fourth lesson was connection. This tension between the dance partners through the connection made for a fun, creative dance like no other. She was so right, and it blew me away. The connection with my partner during the dance changed everything. Connection is where you feel and experience being a part of something supportive. Connection creates an empowering feeling that strengthens us. In dance, connection absorbs and transfers energy.

In the dance, the connection allowed the mechanics of what we needed to do to flow with ease. The focus could rest on the playfulness and creativity of the dance. Meditation plays well into this illustration. When we discover the mechanics of meditating, the connection becomes clearer and quicker as we dance through life.

Jacquie and I went to a dance one evening. We were having fun and doing everything our instructor had taught us. After a couple of songs, someone remarked that we were very good dancers. I laughed because I still felt like a rookie on the dance floor. What they saw were two people who had discovered how to connect on the dance floor. We were playful and creative; we took what we learned and let it flow. The connection made it all work.

Meditation also demands that we learn something. To be able to connect with the Holy Spirit, we need to engage. If we stay passive in the journey, the dance will remain disjointed. We need to be ready and willing to dance the dance of life with the Holy Spirit.

While learning the mechanics of meditation, we discover the abundance of everything available to us. The ego feeds off of scarcity, possession, greed, fear, and anything else that will impede its mandate for self-preservation.

Abundance in the realm of embracing meditation sets a whole new stage. Where do we start in this process? It begins with preparing yourself to take in all that is meant and designed for you. We begin by acknowledging that life is bigger than who we are. We acknowledge that God and the Holy Spirit will be our guides through this journey. We accept what we know to be true.

In setting the stage where our focus is to be placed, we look to abundance and acknowledge the abundance of intimacy with our creator—with no limitations. There is an abundance of understanding and knowledge in the relationship between us, the Holy Spirit, and how the dance works in our lives. An abundance of miracles is waiting to happen through the mystery and wonder of life.

If you have read anything about meditation, you have been given poses, locations, and times that work well. I don't have a set time, place, or position. I embrace meditation in every situation. I might be walking, sitting on the couch, lying in bed at night, waiting at an intersection, or sitting in a lobby before a meeting. It doesn't matter less where you are. There is always the opportunity to set aside blocks of time in your favorite places. Meditation—and this dance within—is as constant and natural as breathing.

I chose five focus points in my meditation. Peace, Gratitude, Blessing, Forgiveness, and Awareness. These five focus points are nothing out of the ordinary, and none of them stand above the others. However, there is seamlessness about them that builds off each other. The blending of these five focus points creates the space to be prepared to face any situation through the eyes of the spirit. The ego no longer determines the outcome. The dance within will take on an amazing new quality as we discover the connection of our spirit to the Holy Spirit and find ourselves being less reactive.

Within the five focuses I call the first one and the last one the "bookends" meaning they set the stage for meditation. Peace is our spiritual longing and awareness is our experience. The practice of Gratitude, Blessing and Forgiveness is what connects the dots.

Peace

The acknowledgment of something beyond oneself begins the journey. Setting the stage to experience the journey embraces peace. How is peace attained? Does it come to us? How do we discover peace? What does it hold in our lives? Are we able to give peace away if there is none within us? Is it possible to not have any peace within us? Isn't peace—no matter how far removed—still within us? Where does one start when peace seems elusive and out of reach? How do I know if peace is residing within me?

Peace is acquired by giving it away. Peace reveals itself as we make the conscious choice to grant it a place to attach itself. By acknowledging that life is beyond the human world that the ego sees, we are inviting the Holy Spirit to journey with us. The Holy Spirit's aim is to bring peace. You will recognize it by acknowledging his existence and his invitation to you. Fear begins to dissipate. Something within us softens and changes how we see the world. In that moment, you have everything available to give away peace.

The stillness within us opens up pathways to discovery. Embracing this peace stirs the mind to choose that which the spirit has always longed.

In my meditative process, I position myself to allow for abundant peace. I am abundant in my capacity to absorb peace, and I contemplate the depth of peace that is desired for my life from the Holy Spirit. There is no restriction of this peace, which I am not sure I can contain. I want as much as is possible for me to hold.

In the process of extending myself to embrace peace, I am able to give peace away. In the moment when my spirit opens the way for the Holy Spirit to receive peace, I am capable of releasing peace. The ego cannot comprehend this action or behavior. It requires faith to allow for this to occur. Faith is not of the ego. The spirit is designed to reach into the well of faith and bring it to the mind. This personal peace will never leave once it is set. The ego will attempt to hide it and make it unimportant, but it cannot take away the peace that holds order in our lives.

The progression of this internal peace reaches out to want more. If I go back to my friend who had his leg cut open, having peace in his mind was far more important than having a leg on which to walk. The internal conflict of no peace is crippling. The consequences of no peace bring circumstances that hold back miracles.

The peace within extends to having peace with the Holy Spirit, and guilt loses its hold. The internal progression of peace and the gift the Holy Spirit extends to all those we encounter throughout the day. We look less and less to be the antagonist. We see our world through a new lens, and the energy we extend becomes reflective to everyone around us.

Extending peace to all of life creates the stage for miracles to unfold. Peace, by its very design, calms agitated souls from which the ego demands allegiance. This level of peace unsettles the ego, and it has no capacity to accept what the Holy Spirit offers: life in exchange for death and faith in exchange for control.

This unfolding of peace permeates the soul, which allows the mind to enlarge its ability to give away peace without restriction. When we extend peace and remove the barriers of antagonism, fear dissipates. Fear holds us back. Peace releases. To know peace is to give away peace.

Gratitude

Our souls are laid bare in the eyes of gratitude. To be grateful is to see that there is abundance of life. Gratitude unlocks the door of the soul to see that there is no restriction within the experiences we encounter.

When we position ourselves in acknowledging gratitude for each and every experience that occurs during the day, we discover a heightened awareness of peace. The experiences could be enjoyable, difficult, crazy, and complicated, but when the mind makes the conscious decision to be grateful, the spirit reminds us to express gratitude in all circumstances.

It is always easier to express gratitude for that which is pleasurable or desirable to us. The change has a remarkable impact when we embrace gratitude in moments when we grit our teeth over something that pushes up against us. In those moments, the Holy Spirit, which has already brought peace to the soul, nudges the spirit to engage the mind to choose differently.

I position myself at the beginning of each day to embrace gratitude for each and every experience that I will encounter. At the end of the day, I show gratitude for what the experiences taught me. It sounds easy to do in the routine of life, but when the world throws a curveball into your world, being grateful is bit more complicated.

Not that many years ago, I experienced one of those moments that pushed me into a place of loss. There seemed to be no answers. One of my best friends was diagnosed with ALS. He was forty. In three years, he went from being fully healthy to becoming a shadow of his physical self. Before he breathed his last breath, I found myself going through phases of mourning and trying to comprehend what he was going through.

As the months progressed—and his body stopped working— it became more evident that his journey was coming to an end. I found myself expressing gratitude for his life, his friendship, our experiences, his zest for life, and his talents, hopes, and dreams. He passed away at forty-three. There were many moments when I found it challenging to express gratitude, but I made a decision to express a thankful soul for the gift of friendship he brought me.

A short time later, I went through the personal loss of my company, my home disappeared, my marriage collapsed, and life spiraled down. The feeling of loss at another level can consume the soul, and a sense of peace is hard to hold on to. The choice to be grateful in this space was sometimes overwhelming. To feel the power of gratitude even when life seems to go against the grain is the power that will be evident by something that is beyond the ego's idea of self-preservation. Something in the spirit stirs, and peace carries you through.

Blessing

What is a blessing? We hear it often. In religious circles, you hear the phrase in different forms, but it basically has the same message: *May peace and blessing be upon your life.*

What does a blessing do? A blessing is a choice we make that opens the space for others to grow. A blessing is like giving a glass of water to the thirsty. It gives life to the soul. In the intentional act of giving voice to a blessing, gratitude manifests itself for the one who is being blessed. Giving a blessing is like giving away peace.

To bless is to pronounce peace. To remove the ego's driven nature and frame guilt on others, the ego must judge. By choosing to bless, judgment diminishes and loses its appeal. The ego cannot find guilt when the foundation of peace—expressed through gratitude—releases blessing. The ego will struggle when it loses its power to be judgmental. To bless is to deposit life into someone's life account.

Forgiveness

Life exists through the measurement of forgiveness. There are no shortcuts to embracing forgiveness. The ego may go along with the idea of forgiveness, but it will place conditions based upon what it believes is acceptable. The ego will consider circumstances, determine what is forgivable, and act according to the standard it measures from.

We marvel when we read or hear stories of someone forgiving a person over a crime that should demand retribution or punishment. How is that person willing to let go of something that has caused such enormous pain? Forgiveness is an all-in, no shortcuts action. The minute we partially forgive, we restrict the possibilities of the manifestation of miracles.

Are we able to see forgiveness as a letting go? To be able to let go of the pain, loss, suffering, or feeling wronged takes more than a determined effort. When the Holy Spirit is embraced as your guide, you have an internal support system to walk you through the process.

As we embrace the gift of peace, life through forgiveness is a life of gratitude and blessing. Forgiveness allows for unlimited miracles. Letting go completely dismantles the ego. To let go is to relinquish any judgments that will bring guilt, no matter who the guilt is directed at.

Guilt has a way of minimizing what forgiveness offers. Holding on to guilt in small ways presumes that guilt is still valuable. The ego has brought to mind that it is not possible to escape guilt. In a guilt-free life, forgiveness carries us. Hold resentment—and watch how your energy drains. Loss, isolation, and loneliness attach themselves when we hold onto that which the ego clings to, preserving what it believes is beneficial and fully knowing that it has you on the path to death.

Imagine filling two buckets with forgiveness. Place one in each hand, and have them ready as you go about your day. Each day provides opportunities to release forgiveness. Sometimes it's as simple as when someone cuts you off. Our reactions can be varied. When a life scenario causes us to cringe, know that forgiveness is at the ready in each hand. We would have to put the buckets down to bring up our fists.

This time element in our mind is where we get to choose whether to go with forgiveness or to fight back. The ego wants to fight back because it can only see defense as its resource. To discover the ability to let go is the most powerful life lesson we can learn. Life challenges and complexities don't stop coming to us, but we have a far greater awareness and ability to let go faster and forgive, which allows blessings to flow, gratitude to be manifested, and peace to be the hallmark of the journey.

Awareness

As we position ourselves to be aware of life around us, we begin to see miracles unfold in ways we never dreamed possible. Awareness creates the space for us to experience life in a conscious state of vibrancy. The more aware we are, the more we recognize when miracles occur. Even more fun, we can anticipate them.

I never ask for miracles anymore; I only ask what part of the miracle I am. The difference may seem subtle, but the experience and outcomes are profound. To be aware of the role one has in miracles opens up possibilities beyond imagination. To not have to concern oneself with miracles is to be at peace. Miracles are occurring every day—and all the time.

What does a miracle look like? Miracles catch us by surprise and cause us to wonder at how circumstances came together to produce the result. All too often, we aren't prepared to experience miracles when they show up. To know we each have roles in miracles is to know that there is something beyond the ego's limited grasp of what is capable in life.

To feel energy come to us and to be released from us as we encounter miracles brings a humility that the spirit can only express as mystery beyond mystery. This connection is the essence of life. Miracles flow through us as we allow ourselves to be positioned to partner into miracles. By letting go of judgments and resentments, paths clear. By blessing others and filling their life accounts, opportunities expand. By demonstrating gratitude, souls flourish. When all this is in full awareness, peace manifests and allows the full expression of our relationship with the Holy Spirit to open up a world where truth resides and purpose takes root.

Jesus had one of those experiences. I often wondered how Jesus could say he only did what he believed the Father was doing and how he positioned himself to be available for miracles to occur. One such story had Jesus was walking through a village with his disciples, rubbing shoulders with the locals as they attempted to get through the crowded streets.

An ill lady thought she would experience a miracle and be healed if she could touch the hem of his garment. She did manage to and was indeed healed. What happened next revealed much about who Jesus was.

Jesus stopped and asked, "Who touched me?"

His friends—somewhat confused by the question—asked, "What do you mean?"

"Can't you see we are all rubbing shoulders? This busy market is crowded." His response captured the attention of the disciples. "Someone touched me, and I felt it."

What did he feel? He knew instantly that energy had been released through and from his body. There was awareness in his spirit. He knew something beyond the norm had occurred.

His friends didn't comprehend what was happening. They were perplexed by what he was telling them.

He said it with enough strength that those around him couldn't avoid hearing it.

The woman humbly came forward and said, "It is I." She thought that she could become well by touching his hem.

Jesus looked at her and smiled. "Your faith has made you well. Go in peace."

Her miracle was affirmed, and her life changed.

His friends were in awe of what happened.

For Jesus, it was a demonstration of what life would be like for those who chose to follow what he was offering. The narrative on Jesus is that he took time to live a life of peace, gratitude, blessing, and forgiveness, which created an awareness of life in spirit. He was not dictated or driven by ego, which is only capable by living in guilt. There is no guilt in the life the Holy Spirit offers.

As we position ourselves to live by the invitation of what the Holy Spirit offers us, we find ourselves embodying peace, gratitude, blessing, forgiveness, and an awareness of life that nothing in the ego is capable of accomplishing. The ego will be dismantled and unable to control your life. It will attempt to continually sabotage the journey, but once the spirit enters into the realm of living with the Holy Spirit as guide, you will find your journey home.

CHAPTER 15

And Finally

This foundation of a meditation process can set the course of life. How do we cope with the stress of a world that presses in on us from all sides? I was reading commentaries that described how we are using mind-altering drugs to cope with life. The reporter was commenting on how half the corporate world is on antidepressants. (Vancouver Sun, December 9, 2013) What is that saying about our world? Self-medication appears to be the order of the day. Why is this happening? It seems that there is a disconnect between what we are chasing in the illusion that life offers and the deep longing to find our true purpose.

When we ignore our connection to the Holy Spirit, we rely on ego to manufacture answers and use some sort of rationale that looks for self-preservation. This self-preserving attitude further accelerates the ego's agenda to remain in isolation and separation, which can only lead to a slow death. If you get there by the ego's self-absorbed, "my way or the highway" approach, it will take you to one place and one place only. Is it no wonder that when we forfeit the potential journey, we find our world medicated to ease the anguish of the pressures in which we find ourselves.

Giving ourselves the gift that the Holy Spirit offers and letting go of our attachments and expectations, changes how we see the world and how we experience it. It is an invitation to live in a place where miracles happen. I find myself meditating on these five focus points because they work. They hold me steady in the midst of what life throws at me. Is life complicated at times? Yes. Is life seemingly unfair at times? Yes. Life is to be experienced fully.

There is another level to the meditation practice where I consider the experiences to which I want to connect. The personal list includes the work we are attracted to, the hobbies, the service, and the connection points we choose to pursue. This list, when tied into that which the spirit is connected, will bring about opportunities specifically orchestrated for the journey. The timing of when life events occur becomes more pronounced. Our gifts and talents weave into this space, and we become oriented to be conduits for miracles. Our gifts and talents were never designed to be controlled by the ego's agenda. This is the ego dictating through fear and separation. The journey asks us to cheer each other along, honor who we are, and support each other as we move through life.

Consider, contemplate, and experience life in ways that are shaped by how we live in spirit. We have explored the questions around guilt and what it looks like, how guilt shapes our decisions, and how guilt motivates us to react to life as it unfolds. As I go about my day, my internal decision-making process can be sabotaged if I perceive some form of threat to my ego. It can happen in a heartbeat. On some levels, we are very fragile human creatures.

Besides asking questions and exploring the idea of guilt, I wanted to be able to give some context about why I believe guilt operates the way it does. I wanted to weave in my understanding of what I think happens as we dig deeper and ask certain questions. How do we pursue life? How is guilt measured by the moral code we carry?

Life has so much more to offer. Our morality defines our mortality, and our mortality defines our morality. You have to think deeply about choosing a moral ethic that is supported by spirit and not just influenced by ego, which is innately limited. The ego-focused world is trapped by the limitations of being human. The spirit within pulls and draws us to see life differently.

My intent has been to shift the story from living under the rule of the ego to the guidance of spirit. This will draw you to a place where the spirit is given the chance to express life and live in a creative, expressive manner that is constantly giving and releasing healing energy. In that place, miracles are encountered and experienced as normally as breathing. I invite you into the world of meditation to focus on a moment-by-moment basis and experience peace, gratitude, blessing, forgiveness, and love. This awareness will keep your inner compass true.

When we learn to live in spirit, the dance within opens us to untold possibilities. Meditation with the Holy Spirit creates the space for miracles to flow. It gives you a solid foundation that is truly reliable to the soul. The mind will be active and engaged in choices that see life beyond our wildest dreams. The giving and receiving of spiritual energy holds us true.

To live in harmony is to be supported and strengthened. To live in tension, the kind I described earlier, is to be one who listens and adjusts to allow the amazing sounds that your life can make.

Allow the spirit the freedom to tap into the timeless, creative, life-giving energy that the Holy Spirit offers. In doing so, the mad idea of how ego uses guilt to motivate life will be transitioned to life—and the spirit will be motivated to live through the abundance of miracles and the connection to the spirit.

Our journey here is filled with complexities, oddities, and struggles that are intertwined and mixed with pleasure and fun. No matter where you find yourself in this journey, embrace it all. Above all, I invite you to journey with the Holy Spirit. You will see how the world is filled with awe and wonder in each and every moment.

Cheers!

Questions for the reader to contemplate

1. Does guilt play a role in life? If so, does it serve us or do we serve it?

2. How quickly do we judge things—no matter how grand or insignificant the thoughts or actions might be?

3. If we need guilt to satisfy the ego, what do we gain from using guilt to journey through life?

4. Does guilt actually assist us in finding out how and why we are here?

5. What is this self that we create to help us maneuver through life?

6. What is our task here on earth?

7. What is it we believe our journey here is about?

8. When we breathe our last breath, what will we understand about life and our experiences here?

9. What does this journey reveal to us about how we find the way home?

10. Guilt will motivate us to do things we internally wrestle with. Peer pressure, family pressure, doctrinal beliefs, and religious beliefs push us toward a place that we don't want to go. Why do we buy into this behavior when we know the outcome will not serve us?

11. How many times have we judged something with very little understanding or grasp of what we are judging?

12. How often have you pursued something in life that you thought mattered, only to discover that what you were chasing was an illusion—something that never gave you what it promised?

13. Miracles are all around us—all the time, constantly. Do we see them? Do we recognize them when they occur?

14. Have we positioned ourselves to be in that place when miracles show up?

15. Does meditation fit into the world of Guilt?

16. How fast are we able to let things go?

17. How do we cope with the stress from a world that presses in on us from all sides?

CPSIA information can be obtained at www.ICGtesting.com
Printed in the USA
LVOW07s0023111214

418209LV00002B/34/P

9 781452 520551